Copyright © 2018 by TEM21 LLC

All rights reserved. This book or any portion thereof may not be reproduced or used in any manner whatsoever without the express permission of the publisher except for the use of brief quotations in a book review or scholarly journal.

First Printing 2018

ISBN 978-1-71612-494-5

TEM21 LLC

4400 Lee Highway, #109

Arlington, VA 22207

USA

Title Page

"Lead, follow, or get out of the way."

Thomas Paine (1738 – 1795)

I have seen this exhortation emblazoned across entrances, stairwells and mess halls in military barracks throughout the English speaking world. I walked, ran and low-crawled under these words daily during my time in the Officer Candidate School at the US Army Infantry Center in Fort Benning, Georgia. That was long, long ago in a universe far, far away.

Most people assume that the words were those of some great historical military leader. I thought the terse order originated in the mists of time from someone like General Sun Tzu, or Emperor Napoleon Bonaparte or General of the Army Douglas MacArthur.

In fact, the originator of this idea was not military at all. These were the words of a British subject and American colonist who was helping foment rebellion in 1776.

In the years leading up to the American Revolution, Thomas Paine was a speaker and writer who devoted himself to criticizing monarchies worldwide. His intent with these particular words was to urge the prominent citizens of the colonies to lead all colonists in a revolt against the tyranny of the British throne.

Paine made the acquaintance of Benjamin Franklin in London in 1774, and moved to Philadelphia shortly before the battles of Lexington and Concord. His best known opinion piece was called *Common Sense* and was published in Philadelphia in 1776 as a pamphlet. It was essentially a condemnation of the rule of monarchs over any free people. He studied world history as far back in time as King David in the Old Testament through Nero in Rome and all the way up to George III in England. His studies led to his passionate belief that the only righteous way for a free people to be governed was by a representative government in a democratic republic. Mr. Paine was adamant that a royal person's birth did not make them a leader.

He saw the nascent rebellion against the rule of King George III as a noble endeavor. His *Common Sense* has been credited with influencing the framers of the US Constitution.

Table of Contents

	Title Page	1
	Table of Contents	3
	Introduction	4
Chapter One	What is Leadership?	9
Chapter Two	Why Lead?	27
Chapter Three	Who should Lead?	36
Chapter Four	How to Lead?	46
Chapter Five	Where to Lead?	57
Chapter Six	When to Lead?	65
	Afterword	66
	References/Resources	68
Appendix A	The Un-Leader	71
Appendix B	Sum of the Psychology Jung	75
Appendix C	Sum of my MBTI results	79
Appendix D	A Theory of Human Motivation	84

Introduction

I am writing this book to share with you the experience and knowledge that I have accrued over the last forty years as a small unit leader in the military and in business. Doing anything for that long creates a great deal of perspective. I am attempting to put that perspective to good use by blending experience and knowledge into a guide for aspiring small unit leaders. This guide is carefully grounded in a common sense approach to all things.

Veteran's Administration statistics indicate that since the end of the Vietnam War (and the attendant end of the draft) less than seven per cent of the US population has entered the US military services. Therefore, it follows that over 90 per cent of the US population has not had the opportunity to gain the basic skills, knowledge and abilities needed to lead by way of the tried and true "military model", as it is called in academia.

You should read this book because life is too short to learn from your own experience alone. This book is about real, day-to-day, practical leadership in small units or teams of any kind. There are excellent and well researched text books that convey information and theories of leadership but they do not convey reality or practicality. These are gained only through experience and practice.

I have led (and been led by) some of the best and some of the worst. My twenty years in the Army happened to include direct contact with a five star General of the Army and a Command Sergeant Major who both fought and led in World War II. Conversely, I led some of the last draftees in the US Army. I see Arlington National Cemetery as the Camelot of military leadership and sacrifice. We all see monuments to fallen police and firefighters in the same light. For that matter, there is now an orbiting red sports car that attests to visionary leadership in industry.

After my retirement, I was a founding partner of a small business that operated profitably for 16 years in the areas of Information Technology and Security. We were a small group of professionals who deployed to more than 30 foreign countries on a continual basis. We acquired a strong reputation for timely, effective action on tasks that were almost always performed under difficult circumstances.

In this guide, I offer the benefit of one small unit leader's experience. I intend to expedite your pursuit of success as a sensible, effective small unit leader. Small units are groups of people who are joined together to accomplish clearly defined tasks, objectives or functions. Inevitably, small unit leaders grow and advance to become the sensible, effective senior leaders and executives in larger organizations.

This book is a blend that is drawn from three vats. The first consists of military leadership doctrine as published in several documents. I transform and translate the contents of those documents into terminology that is more understandable and more applicable to the civilian environment. The second vat draws upon existing literature in academia and in business about leadership and management. Last, I add to this body of knowledge my own experience and the lessons I have learned as a small unit leader for about 40 years in both military and civilian environments.

I believe that one thing I have learned from all three of these sources is that leadership is a thing unto itself. It is a combination of art and science that is practiced and learned on a continual basis. Leadership is the critical catalyst that produces success in any group endeavor in any unit or team. Success in small units, of course, aggregates to become success in large organizations.

Thomas Paine was right that leaders are not born but rather they are made. Witness a group of high school students from Margaret Stoneman who have been forged into leaders virtually overnight by their own suffering and loss.

In 2015, General Stan McChrystal, et al, published their book entitled *Team of Teams*. In the book they asserted that it is necessary for large organizations to adapt to their operational environment and circumstances in order to function effectively. They provided a well-researched description of the long standing emphasis on efficiency that came to be known as scientific management. It was introduced early in the industrial revolution by Frederick W. Taylor. Scientific management emphasized a pursuit of ultimately efficient processes in organizations of all sizes. Efficiency was blindly pursued through processes and organizational structures that were hierarchical and inflexible to the point of being ineffective.

The authors of *Team of Teams* compared and contrasted the processes and practices of small, focused teams against those of the larger parent organizations to which those teams belonged as subordinate elements. They looked at military, commercial and governmental teams and organizations. They concluded that well led unit level teams were much better able to be adaptive and flexible in their efforts to be effective in changing environments and circumstances. Whereas, larger organizations were structured in a way that adaptation was very difficult or impossible.

Chapter One

What is leadership?

"Leadership is the art of getting someone else to do something you want done because he wants to do it. "

President Dwight Eisenhower (1890 – 1969)

I know that leadership is an art because it comes from the heart. Leaders selflessly fulfill their responsibilities to accomplish their tasks, objectives and functions. They are devoted to their responsibilities to motivate and support their people. Effective leaders focus first on these responsibilities and last on the authority and power that might accompany them.

Sun Tzu was a famous and successful general in ancient China. He led several armies during feudal warfare among Chinese city-states around 1500 BC. The lessons he and his fellow generals learned during their exploits have been compiled in a small but powerful book called the *Art of War*. It has long been mandatory reading for military leaders and more recently for business leaders as well. Note that the book was not titled *'Management of War'* or *'Pondering War'*.

"Lead people, manage things".

Rear Admiral Grace Hopper (1906 -1992)

In our modern world, leadership is an art that requires a mix of science as well. You will soon learn that Admiral Hopper's advice is axiomatic. Management is a necessary adjunct skill for effective leaders.

You will lead people and you will manage things. The people you will lead will come in all sizes, shapes, colors and creeds.

The most regimented military organizations that for millennia were homogeneous groups of men are largely gone. The detrimental effects of historical prejudices based on race, gender or other personal characteristics are leaving our society and our military as well.

The things that you will manage are also many and varied:

Time is definitely the scarcest and most pressing thing you will need to manage. The clock will tick forward at exactly one second per second. There will be times when you will want it to slow down. There will be other times when you will wish very strongly that it speed up. You will get exactly 24 hours each day – no more, no less. Like money, time can be wasted or it can be invested. It can be used wisely or frittered away. As a small unit leader, you will operate on relatively short timelines. Your approach to time management will need to be tightly linked with your operational priorities. The things that will take the longest will need to be started first. The things that will need to be synchronized with other actions will need to be arranged accordingly. The simple adage of 'first things first' will succeed for you most of the time.

Money is the thing that you might tend to focus on first and most. That would be a mistake. Money will not grow on trees, but it can be generated when necessary. It can be borrowed, raised and allocated cautiously. You will need to tightly link financial management to your operational planning. It will fail the common sense test to plan something that cannot be funded. Conversely, limited financial assets should never be an excuse for not carrying on the job as best it can be done within the funding available.

Equipment and facilities will be constrained as well. You will need to know your assets thoroughly. You will also need to know how to use those assets. You cannot be a 'suit' who will manage from afar. You will need to know how to show your people how to use the unit's assets when necessary. You will need to chip in and make sure the job gets done even if you are the only one there to continue the work. Captains of Fire Companies will always know how to operate a hose and drive a truck.

Technology will be ubiquitous. You should view technology as a tool that supports your unit's objectives and makes your people more effective and efficient than they would otherwise be.

> I interpreted Stanley Kubrick's mysterious monolith in his 1968 movie *2001: A Space Odyssey* as an icon for the continual and perpetual advancement of technology. The monolith's first appearance in the movie coincided with the image of the leader of a troop of pre-human bipeds arguing with another troop about which group would get to eat the remains of a rotting carcass. The leader of the first troop reached down and grabbed the thighbone from the carcass and bashed the opposing troop leader in the head, ending the argument once and for all. I saw this as representing the first implementation of

technology in the form of a weapon. The next time the monolith appeared, mankind had jumped into space exploration.

Leadership is an art that is highly situational. As an art, leadership is practiced in order to achieve some defined purpose. Science is a body of knowledge that can be possessed, remembered, held and still be of value. A body of knowledge is a passive thing, until it is acted upon. Knowledge can be stored for long periods of time and then accessed for whatever purpose is at hand. The Dead Sea scrolls hold knowledge that sat dormant for millennia before being discovered and advancing science.

You must practice the art of leadership kinetically. Picasso had to take a brush and use it to apply paint to the canvas in order to produce an object for others to see and appreciate. You must actively apply your knowledge, skills and abilities to motivate others, solve problems and make decisions.

There are no dormant leaders. If you are dormant you are either following or getting out of the way. There is not necessarily anything wrong with either of those. You need followers in order to be a leader. The best small unit leaders are generally good followers as well.

Following can be a productive thing to do, as is getting out of the way sometimes, depending on the situation.

The situation guides a leader about the best way to lead others. Let me illustrate:

> Some years ago, I stood in front of a squad of 11 young soldiers. It was my responsibility to lead them through a set of very basic tasks such as walking in a straight line, marching in step with each other and occasionally changing directions. We also changed the rifles we were carrying from one shoulder to the other. In this situation the small unit consisted of people with some high school diplomas and some General Educational Development (GED) certificates. Although I did not know it at the time, one of them was actually a member of a sub-population of soldiers called McNamara's Hundred Thousand. Robert McNamara was the US Secretary of Defense from 1961 through 1968 during much of the Vietnam War. He instituted a policy in 1966 of permitting the military to enlist young men who had Intelligence Quotients (IQ's) that were appreciably below average (10 – 30 percentile). The maximum number to be granted enlistment with those IQ's was nominally limited to 100,000. However, it is estimated to have

actually been as high as 350,000. Unfortunately, the Vietnam War required a continuing source of manpower.

The only effective way for me to lead that small unit to perform those tasks in that situation was to issue clear, concise orders with which the eleven soldiers complied immediately without any analysis, discussion or hesitation. This was an authoritative style of leadership. It was the correct style of leadership in that situation. We were not an intellectual powerhouse but we got from point A to point B as required. We did so many times.

Similar situations occur in a football game when the quarterback decides what play to run and communicates that very concisely to the team in the huddle. When the ball is hiked, every member of the team executes their assigned task without any deep analysis, discussion or hesitation. If you watch a choreographer instruct a dance troupe on how to perform a dance routine, you will see very little analysis and lots of concise, authoritative instructions.

When a fire department responds to a fire alarm in an office building, they immediately assess the situation and then issue orders concerning evacuation and the deployment of fire-fighting equipment and first responders. In that situation, an authoritative approach is what is needed and is what produces the best results.

More recently, I led another small unit consisting of 18 information technology professionals. It was my responsibility to lead them on a project to design, engineer and test a complex telecommunications system that would operate at 60 sites in 33 countries. It would span most of the western hemisphere. Our group collectively possessed a dozen undergraduate degrees, a half dozen graduate degrees and two Ph. D.'s. We were a diverse group of people with very different backgrounds and highly specialized skills.

This situation was quite different from the squad of soldiers I led earlier. The tasks at hand were much more complex and challenging. This small unit did not consist of a group of young people who were lined up in the same uniforms and expecting to hear orders and comply without any analysis, discussion or hesitation.

The style of leadership that was appropriate for this second small unit was a collegial one. We were, in fact, colleagues. We all had something valuable and important to contribute to the project. At some points in our efforts the de-facto leadership changed from me to one of the other people who held the most knowledge or skill in a particular subject. That person's gender, race or religious preferences were absolutely irrelevant. I felt no need to assert myself as the leader at that point. It was very productive to relegate the matter of 'who is in charge' below the matters of 'what' and 'how' to best address a challenge.

You will need to assess the situations in which you lead and then apply the approach that fits best. Assessing the situation should be based on common sense and an emphasis on what needs to be accomplished, who is on the team doing it and the circumstances surrounding the effort. These circumstances will include things like people, time, material, weather, safety, etc.

The styles of leadership lay along a continuum that has authoritarian at one extreme and collegial at the other. The gradations between usually consist of a combination of the two. The midpoint of this continuum of styles or approaches is often called collaborative. This is illustrated in Figure 1, below.

Collaborative leadership is a way of leading through the use of ideas and suggestions that are derived from all of the members of the unit. The leader acts like a moderator who starts a discussion of different ideas, approaches and recommendations on how the unit should proceed on some given endeavor. After a thorough discussion and analysis by all the members in the unit, the leader decides which alternative that was discussed is to be executed. Actions that are premised upon collaborative decisions like this tend to be carried out with greater enthusiasm and commitment by the unit overall.

There is a caution that you will need to observe when using the collaborative approach. A phenomenon called 'Group Think' needs to be avoided. This term was coined after a poor decision was made by President John F Kennedy concerning a Central Intelligence Agency operation called the Bay of Pigs in 1961.

President Kennedy made a decision to support an amphibious landing by exiled Cuban patriots who wanted to overthrow the recently installed communist government of Fidel Castro. The collaborative decision process failed to include all relevant facts and the analysis overlooked glaring problems that ended up foiling the operation.

You are unlikely to determine the fate of amphibious invasions of sovereign countries, but you do need to be smart and make sure collaborative decisions do not turn into cheerleading sessions. You will need to ensure that a cool, rational analysis of the alternatives is completed.

As I think back over myriad decisions, problems and leadership challenges, I would estimate that the distribution of my uses of different leadership styles approximates a bell curve as illustrated in Figure 1 below. I most often found some type of collaboration to be effective and useful. Collaboration would constitute the large area under the middle of the bell curve. The number of times I led authoritatively were few and far between and could be seen as the small left side tail of the bell curve. Likewise, I did use the collegial approach during several efforts that called for it. These would be depicted as the small right tail of the bell curve. It is also true that your style as a leader will change over time as you gain more experience with people and with situations.

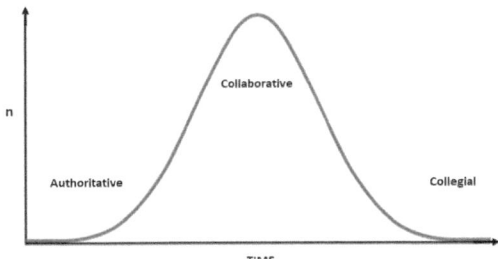

Figure 1 Leadership Styles

What is a small unit? In a professional sense, a small unit is a group of people who are joined together to accomplish a clearly defined task, objective or function. The number of people in a small unit can vary from two to about 50. Some times the number might exceed 50, but not often.

The ultimate small unit in our society, of course, has always been the family. Back in the day (meaning from ancient times up until recently) a family consisted of an alpha male father, a beta female mother and some number of offspring. That is no longer the case in our society, now or in the future. A contemporary family often consists of a mother and a child or two. It may have only a father and one child. It may have two mothers and children or two fathers and a child. No matter what the composition of a family it remains a unit. As such, it needs leadership. Women lead family units all over the world every day. Fathers follow the lead of mothers by staying home while she earns the bread. Parents of any gender are now collaborating to lead family units. These fundamental shifts in the composition of families may be frightening to some, but they are very encouraging to others.

I see the change as representing the future of the family unit. It is a new and different situation that must be assessed and an appropriate leadership style applied that supports the best results for all family members in any given situation. These shifts are recent enough that they have not produced a large amount of empirical data to analyze with regard to outcomes.

Leadership is an art that you will practice in a group setting, but it will be a very personal art. You will learn this forcefully the first time you sit down in front of a group of people who need to be led. Their eyes will communicate silent questions and expectations. They will expect you to provide answers. Sometimes no words will be spoken. Expectations will be made clear by the situation and the readiness of people to follow.

Teachers often appreciate the lights that go on in a student's eyes when they actually grasp and learn something. So you, as a leader, can derive great satisfaction and self-motivation when the eyes and actions of your people make it clear they know exactly what to do and how to do it because you were there to guide them.

You will be tempted to succumb to the frills and accoutrements of leadership. It will be important to avoid anything that accrues to your personal advantage by virtue of your leadership position.

The authority that you will have as a leader will be a very exciting thing. Authority will equal power. However, the excitement will be as fleeting as will be the power. A person's ego can be easy to inflate, but it can be even easier to deflate. You will be better off using what little power you may have (small unit leaders get small amounts of power, after all) to the benefit of the unit and the people in it.

When I was a senior executive of a small company, I had some amount of power over hiring, firing, salary, bonus, etc. It was also true that when the cleaning crew did not empty the trash for some reason, I was the one who emptied it into the dumpster at the end of the day. You will need to concentrate on the fulfillment of your responsibilities first and exercising authority last and only when necessary.

In Appendix A, you will find a description of what I describe as the *Un-leader*. That is the person who fails to prioritize responsibility over authority. You should not be that person.

Let's discuss that **vision** thing. You will be better served by clear focus on the actual situation on the ground when and where you are operating. Vision will become a valuable leadership tool at the upper levels of executive leadership and management. It will have much less relevance in a small shop that needs to get a specific number of new tires mounted and balanced on customers' cars within the next three days. The day before opening night of a community play, the director, staff and actors will need to focus very keenly on their readiness to entertain a group of people very soon. On December 22nd, vision won't help a loading dock supervisor get all of the packages on the 6 trucks that are still running and delivered safely before the holidays (or the weather) intervene.

You will operate at what economists call the 'micro-level' of our economy/society. You will be in a small unit doing relatively small things over a relatively small area. You will need to focus on the matter(s) at hand. You will need to lead a small group of people to use a limited set of things to do what is **necessary**. You will seldom get to do things that are nice or other than the **necessary**. You will need to focus on here, now and a bit into the future.

Your future vision is really just thinking ahead to tomorrow or maybe next week. If you start getting all visionary, tires don't get balanced correctly and cause accidents. If you allow your focus to shift too far into the future, delivery trucks get overloaded and head out on impassable, icy roads with disastrous results.

A good thing for you to remember is that it is really only superman who leaps tall buildings in a single bound. The rest of us get over tall buildings (or difficult obstacles) by realizing that we should stick with getting to the top of an obstacle one step at a time or at least in stages. Complex tasks will be best addressed in a fashion that breaks them down into more basic components that can be addressed using the right combination of people and things.

Conversely, you should handle simple matters in simple ways. I have found that things are as simple as you let them be.

I found some other book definitions of leadership that warrant listing, as follows:

"Webster's Dictionary" defines leadership as -

- Guiding on a way, especially by going in advance
- Directing on a course or in a direction
- Directing the operations, activity or performance of
- To have charge of
- To go at the head of
- To be first in or among

Wikipedia provides this very terse definition of leadership –

- Influencing others

The US Army Leadership Field Manual (FM) 6-22 defines leadership as -

- The process of influencing people by providing purpose, direction and motivation while operating to accomplish the mission and improving the organization

Introduction to Leadership – Concepts and Practice provides a multi-faceted definition of leadership, as follows:

- Leadership is different things to different people based on studies of leadership and leaders. Leadership is described as a set of traits, abilities, skills, behaviors and relationships.

Chapter Two

Why lead?

"The key is not to make quick decisions, but to make timely decisions."

General Colin Powell

You will lead because leadership is necessary whenever two or more people engage in any endeavor together. You may very simply be appointed as the leader of a small unit within a large organization; or you may decide to become an entrepreneur and lead your own small company. There are many ways to either find yourself in a leadership role, or to voluntarily assert yourself as the leader of a small group, unit or team.

In any case, you will find that the nucleus of your activities will be making decisions. Regardless of whether the style of leadership you use is authoritarian, collaborative or collegial, you will soon be called upon to make decisions. You will own your decisions and the results that they produce.

You will need to make decisions because they are necessary in order for action to be initiated. No leader, no decisions, no actions. Absent leadership, stagnation and/or chaos will result. The basic law of inertia will take over. Bodies at rest will remain at rest while bodies in motion will remain in motion (probably the wrong motion in the wrong direction). Small unit leaders must be action oriented.

Of course, there is an exception which proves this rule. Sometimes the best decision to make is no decision, or to do nothing. This 'null alternative' is often overlooked.

Sometimes you will need to face multiple decisions rapidly. Other times you will need to consider a large array of information and try to derive from it the best decision. Decisions can be arrived at individually or in a group. As with leadership in general, the right decision process will be situational.

You will make lots of decisions. Some will be easy while others will be very complex. Some will be required to solve problems while others will be required to avert problems. No matter how collaborative a decision might have been during the process of reaching it, it will finally come to be yours. You will learn this about five minutes after you make your first bad decision. Those who will have cheered you on to the right decision will be the first to remind you that the 'final decision' will be yours - and it will be. Bearing responsibility for decisions will be part of the leadership territory.

You will find many suggested methodologies for decision making. I would recommend that you adopt a modified, more relaxed version of the rigid military model. You will face your first decision very soon in your tenure as a small unit leader. It will not come in a vacuum. You may need to make several decisions simultaneously and quickly.

It will be important that you approach all of your decisions in an objective, rational way. In order to do so, you will need to pay close attention to Step 1, below (which is my own modification).

Step 1: Remain calm.

This will be critical. In order to make a sound, correct decision you will need to avoid the very frequent mistake of jumping to conclusions and actions without first being certain that you have a clear understanding of what the problem is and what decision is really required.

Step 2: Recognize and define the problem and/or decision.

You cannot solve a problem or make a decision if you are not aware that the need exists. You should encourage your people to be open and forthcoming about the situation surrounding your unit's efforts to accomplish its objectives. You yourself should be ever vigilant and aware of your operational environment. You will need to be sure you address the real problem or decision that is required, rather than the apparent or perceived issue.

Step 3: Gather facts related to the problem and/or decision.

You will need to gather objective, rational facts and information surrounding the problem or decision that you are addressing. Sound decisions will never be based on false or incomplete information.

Step 4: Develop alternative decisions and/or solutions.

There will seldom be only one alternative way to address any issue. If nothing else, you should at least consider what I call the *'null alternative'* of doing nothing.

Step 5: Analyze and compare/contrast alternative decisions and/or solutions.

You will again need to emphasize an objective, rational approach to considering the alternatives. Gut feelings and intuition should be given very minor weight in this analysis.

Step 6: Choose an alternative and implement it.

You will be tempted to become bogged down in a sort of 'paralysis by analysis.' You should avoid this and make a clear, well supported, choice of how to proceed and then act to do what has been decided. A decision that is not implemented will be a wasted decision and will usually end up causing follow-on problems and/or decisions

Step 7: Analyze the decision and/or solution after implementation.

You should assume nothing. You will need to check into the effectiveness of your decision and/or solution after implementation. Be sure it is **done**.

Believe it or not, I have seen the above process followed successfully in a matter of minutes. You and your situation will not likely require that kind of urgency, but it may. I have also seen the process take months to complete. As with leadership itself, your situation will determine how often and how urgently you will need to make decisions. First responders may need to go through this process daily, while someone who is leading a mail room staff might not need to do it very often, or urgently, at all.

Any honest discussion of decisions must address mistakes. You will most certainly make bad decisions and mistakes. Your people will do the same. Mistakes will occur just as the tide will ebb and flow every day. Some mistakes will turn out to be preventable. You will not be able to control one hundred per cent of your circumstances or environment. You will, however, be able to control more of them than you realize. You will have the ability to think ahead and plan so as to avert most mistakes and/or problems. Even the weather will be predicted every day (with arguable accuracy perhaps).

I have always found the pursuit of **perfection** to be pointless. Instead, I have seen the most fruitful approach to quality (of decisions, of products, of processes etc.) as being an insistence on **excellence**.

Perfection generally has been illusory. Pursuit of it has consumed more time, effort and resources than warranted. In many cases, the delivery of a perfect solution too late has been the same as not delivering a solution at all.

Excellence, on the other hand, is a level of quality that can be achieved on a consistent basis. I believe that perfection frequently turns out to be the intersection of excellence and luck. This can be seen in any number of examples in athletics and in art.

When I have been faced with these inevitable mistakes over the years, I have found the following mental framework to be very useful in keeping mistakes less disruptive and more constructive than they might otherwise have been:

First, you must admit the mistake. Whether it is your own or someone else's in your unit, you need to face up to it and own it. History abounds with stories about minor mistakes that turned into major catastrophes simply because they were not acknowledged soon after they occurred.

Second, you should correct the mistake, to the extent that you can. This is not always possible, but many times it will be. An apology and a credit to a customer's bill will be a small effort that can pay large benefits. A mistake on an employee's paycheck should be corrected immediately. Most mistakes in the commercial environment will allow for some sort of correction.

Third, you and your unit need to learn from the mistake. Regardless of whether or not you were able to correct the mistake, it will need to be taken into account in improving the way you will operate in the future. Your efforts to think ahead to minimize mistakes will need to include a careful analysis of past mistakes. History will always be informative.

You should keep your approach to leadership free of egotistical closed-mindedness. I have seen it derail the decision making process in many units and teams over many years.

A closed-minded attitude on the part of a leader is usually based on their egotistical idea that they have already thought of everything. They see no need to consider situations with a fresh perspective and to seek out new facts, information or alternatives. A healthy dose of humility is important for all leaders at all levels.

You should avoid the adage that "there is nothing new under the sun". The sun will rise anew every day. You will need to adopt the approach that nothing will be guaranteed, but anything will be possible.

Chapter Three

Who should lead?

"Leaders are not born, they are developed".

Vince Lombardi (1913 – 1970)

Gordon Gekko was wrong. Greed is not good – especially when it shows up as a principal motivator for someone who seeks to be a leader.

Franklin Delano Roosevelt was right. "The only thing we have to fear is fear itself "– especially when it shows up as the other principal motivator for a would-be leader.

Genuine leaders at all levels are motivated by selflessness and personal courage. They never permit themselves to be motivated by greed and/or fear, ever.

It would be irresponsible to say that just anyone can or should lead. That just is not the reality. It is true, however, that the principal motivators of selflessness and personal courage can be present in anyone regardless of gender, race, color, creed or economic background.

The basic human equation of *'nature + nurture'* applies to the matter of who can and should lead. Everyone is born with a set of inherited traits and characteristics. That is the *'nature'* part of the equation. These traits and characteristics come to us via heredity and basically represent the hand of cards that we are dealt at the outset of life. The *'nurture'* half of the equation refers to how that original hand of cards is played. During our early lives, the cards are played for us by our family, our teachers and others in our close environment. In the final analysis, the cards are played by us for the most part.

Historically, during the long periods of formal, institutional racism in the US military, effective and even heroic leaders arose who were other than white males. Women and minorities from all walks of life became wartime leaders. Japanese-Americans left internment camps and went into battle during WWII in Europe where they won many distinctions for bravery and honor. The Tuskegee Airmen were second to none in their combat success over North Africa, Italy and Central Europe.

Leadership potential was, and is, the key. Leadership potential has proven to be more wide spread than was once believed. Historically, measuring that potential was a very subjective process that was based on social class, financial standing and family lineage. In 1953, a more objective way to gauge the natural potential of a person was established, in the form of the Myers-Briggs Type Indicator (MBTI).

The MBTI questionnaire was based upon the work of a pioneering psychologist – Dr. Carl Gustav Jung (1875 – 1961). Jung managed to penetrate and understand the deepest and most powerful psychological forces in people. A summary of Carl Jung's background and his research is included in Appendix B below.

The MBTI has been a tool used in countless formal leadership development programs world-wide. MBTI assessments have been completed on literally millions of examinees over more than 60 years. Its results and analyses have been proven to be very accurate and reliable. For example, The US Military Academy at West Point has long used the MBTI in its world-renowned leadership program.

The MBTI uses a word association questionnaire to discern the basic psychological traits of those who participate in the assessment. Specifically, it attempts to define a personality type based on four innate personal preferences:

Does a person prefer to focus on the outer world or on their own inner world?

    Extraversion (E) or Introversion (I).

Does a person prefer to focus on the basic information taken in or prefer to interpret and add meaning?

    Sensing (S) or Intuition (N).

When making decisions, does a person prefer to first look at logic and consistency or first look at the people and special circumstances?

    Thinking (T) or Feeling (F).

In dealing with the outside world, does a person prefer to get things decided or do they prefer to stay open to new information and options?

    Judging (J) or Perceiving (P).

A person's personality type is established by their preference in each category. It can be expressed by combining the letters of the preferences in each of the four categories.

There are 16 four-letter codes corresponding to the personality types, as shown below.

ISTJ	ISFJ	INFJ	INTJ
ISTP	ISFP	INFP	INTP
ESTP	ESFP	ENFP	ENTP
ESTJ	ESFJ	ENFJ	ENTJ

The MBTI can help us understand the *'nature'* part of the equation that prospective leaders possess through heredity. Small unit leaders will need to be *'nurtured'* (or *'nurture'* themselves) to control their innate personality characteristics and to develop a clear set of traits in order to succeed as small unit leaders.

The nature of the MBTI personality grid is such that there is no one personality type that is superior to the others as an indicator of leadership potential. Different personality types indicate a higher potential to lead in different situations. An individual's personality type identifies areas where they need to focus their efforts to become leaders through the *'nurturing'* process.

Appendix C is a summary of my own MBTI results for illustration.

Historically, the military has served as a sort of societal petri dish of leadership and small unit leaders. In the United States, the epicenter of that body of knowledge has been, and remains, the leadership program at The US Military Academy at West Point. The Army has documented the gamut of personal traits that have defined effective small unit leaders over the annals of time. The gurus of military leadership have concluded that leaders must acquire the following traits through formal training and/or personal development, practice and experience. The military terminology and frame of reference have been specific to military training and combat leadership. I have attempted to faithfully take this combined wisdom, knowledge and experience with leaders in small military units and reformulate it into more generic terms. The following traits of leadership have proven to apply universally to all small units that exist throughout our society.

Courage is the trait that will make you take necessary risks. It will cause you to be action oriented and to be firm in stressful situations. You will be able to stand up for what is right regardless of what others may think. You will always be willing to accept personal responsibility.

Selflessness will focus you on meeting the needs of your people before your own. You will always share hardships and discomfort with your people. You will take every measure possible to provide for the welfare of your people.

Bearing will enable you to look the part of a leader. It will enable you to control extremes of emotion in your voice, gesture or actions (except at certain times that you carefully choose).

Decisiveness will guide you to study your alternatives and carefully select the best course of action. It will cause you to make decisions quickly when necessary. It will help you know when the null alternative of not making a decision is the right one.

Dependability will make you be where you need to be when you need to be there and to fulfill all tasks and responsibilities in a timely manner.

Endurance will enable you to keep up the physical and mental stamina to lead under stressful conditions and for extended periods of time.

Enthusiasm will help you to always communicate with a positive attitude to your people. You will find it easy to emphasize your people's successes. You will be ready to explain to your people the importance of the tasks and jobs that you expect them to perform. You will regularly encourage your people to overcome obstacles rather than being held by them.

Humility will cause you to insure your people receive the credit when they perform well. You will easily emphasize the importance of each person to the group. You will always describe your unit's performance in terms of "we" rather than "I".

Humor will allow your people to see that you have fun doing your job. You will be able to maintain the ability to joke when the going gets tough.

Initiative will prompt you to take action when something must be done, even without direction from above. You will find it easy to look for and figure out better ways to do things. You will naturally think ahead and plan ahead.

Integrity will compel you to tell the truth and to use your power to gain progress for your people, not for your own gain. It will also help you to encourage honest and open communication among your people. An effective leader will always regard their word to be their bond.

Judgment will help you to consider alternatives before you act and to think out the consequences of what you're about to do before you do it.

Fairness will be your guide in applying rewards and rebukes to all your people consistently. Rewards will best be done in public, while rebukes will be more effective when done in private. It will drive you to make decisions taking into account the well-being of your people as well as job requirements. You will consistently listen to all sides of any issue before making a decision that affects your people

Knowledge will cause you to make reasonable and sound daily operating decisions. It will also enable you to recognize and correct inadequate performance and to demonstrate to your people how they should perform their jobs.

Tact will permit you to speak to others with the same kind of respect that you expect yourself.

Loyalty will drive you to carry out difficult tasks without any complaint and to defend your people against unfair treatment.

Chapter Four

How to lead?

"Common sense is very uncommon"

Horace Greeley (1811 – 1872)

Common sense will be the best guide as you lead your people and manage your things. Your people will need motivation. They will look for you to provide it. The most common sense oriented (and most widely accepted) description of the psychology of human motivation is Professor Abraham H. Maslow's (1908 – 1970) *"A Theory of Human Motivation"*. The gist of the paper has been widely known as 'Maslow's Hierarchy.' I have included his paper in its entirety at Appendix D.

Maslow's theory is that human needs exist in a hierarchy that starts at its lowest, most basic level with *physiological needs* and climbs up through five strata to *self-actualization*. This hierarchy is most frequently depicted as a pyramid, but I view it as a stairway instead. See Figure 2 below.

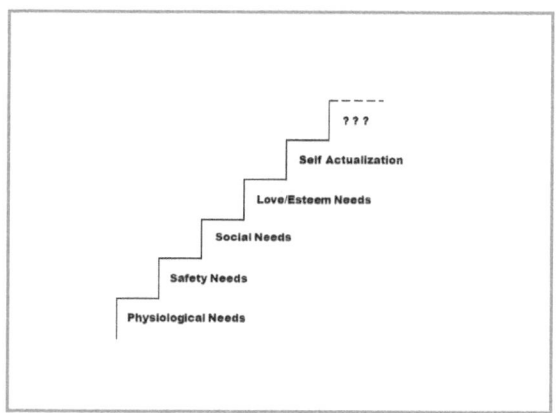

Figure 2 Another View of Maslow's Hierarchy of Need

You will find that your people will respond best to your efforts to motivate them if you keep this hierarchy in mind. You will have a great deal of control over the full range of things that that your people need. You can ensure that your people have the time and resources they need to take care of their own (and their families') needs for physiological support like shelter, food, medical care and transportation. You will be directly responsible for providing and maintaining a safe workplace. You will have the opportunity on a daily basis to either foster or impede social interaction between the people in your unit as a tightly knit team. You can take affirmative action to build the esteem of your people individually and as a team. Small unit leaders will need to be very much committed to the '**all for one and one for all**' ethos.

Self-actualization will really have two levels of meaning to you as a small unit leader. At some point, you will need to help members of your unit to excel to the point where they will need to take on new roles within the unit or elsewhere. Their self-actualization could become your loss. However, you will find that these losses become a matter of pride over time.

The other aspect of self-actualization is one that many leaders will have to deal with at some point. Specifically, what will come next for you after self-actualization?   In larger organizations this might be dealt with straight-forwardly through the process of promotion and advancement. In smaller units, such as small businesses, a successful leader may need to seek another form of advancement. It seems to me that a logical next level above self-actualization might be a need to help others to self-actualize. This might be done in an academic setting or in a less formal mentoring and training mode.

A cautionary note concerning Professor Maslow's Hierarchy – this stairway (as I view it) can go in both directions. You can ascend and you can descend among its levels. Successful leaders will have the best interests of their people in mind at all times and use **common sense communication** to gauge where on the hierarchy a person might be at any given point in time.

What does **common sense communication** look like? It looks like six common sense questions, as follows:

What?

Why?

Who?

How?

Where?

When?

"The manager asks how and when; the leader asks what and why."

Professor Warren Bennis

The first two questions will anchor all leadership communications. You will need to ask them in that order. The other four can be asked in whatever order will seem sensible given the answers to the first two. The implication of Professor Bennis' statement that leaders must be **results oriented** has been borne out many times in my own experience.

When you visit your people while they are engaged in their work, you should always start a discussion with the simple, straightforward question along the lines of "What are we up to at the moment?" You should be prepared for a response along the lines of "Nothing." or "We don't know." They might alternatively respond with exactly what they are doing. In either case, you should respond with "Why?" This will start a dialogue that will always be beneficial in the end. Activities that may have been neglected or were unclear can be corrected before they go completely off track. People who are performing correctly can always benefit from some accolades or encouragement about the importance of what they are doing.

When you think about it, all questions are derived from these six common sense questions.

> "Meanings are not in words, meanings are in people."
>
> S.I. Hiakawa (1906 – 1992)

You will need to be careful that your communications with your people are actually bi-directional. You should avoid the trap of lecturing, ordering, directing and other wise *transmitting* without ever *receiving*. It may interest you to know that it is impossible to listen at the same time you are talking. Remember that it is your responsibility as a leader to ensure that your people end up understanding what you intended to get across.

You should avoid meaningless meetings. You should emphasize common sense communications in group settings just as in one-on-one situations. In a small unit or team, meetings should be few and far between. Instead, frequent working sessions that are focused on specific issues or coordinating instructions will usually bear more fruit. When a formal meeting is actually required, it should have a well-defined purpose and should last only as long as is necessary to achieve that purpose.

The following principles have proven useful in guiding generations of small unit leaders to be more effective. They have been drawn from the leadership program at the US Military Academy in West Point, but they apply universally in all environments.

- Know yourself and seek constant self-improvement. Emulate good leaders around you.
- Be proficient in the tasks involved in your unit's basic functions.
- Take responsibility for your actions and the actions of your people. Correct errors and laud excellence in a timely fashion.
- Make clear and timely decisions when they are required.
- Set the example for your people in all areas of performance and attitude.
- Know your people and look out for their welfare.
- Keep your people informed so they can understand the importance of their work, thereby developing trust in you as a leader.
- Develop a sense of responsibility in your people by empowering them to be independent when and where it is appropriate.
- Monitor performance on a continual basis in order to keep in touch with your people and their performance.

- Develop and improve the competence and performance of your people on a continuing basis. Train your people individually and as teams.
- Operate your unit in accordance with its capabilities, including an element of challenge as well.

Common sense communications will be equally useful as you carry out your responsibility to manage your things as well as to lead your people. Management will consist of the processes of planning, organizing, directing and controlling the activities of an operational unit or team to accomplish a defined set of goals and objectives. See Figure 3 below.

- You will plan by setting specific, achievable objectives and defining the best way to accomplish them. Your planning must remain oriented on practical, operational priorities. You should avoid the syndrome of the **'Grand Planner'**. You will lead a small group with a limited set of resources and a limited time horizon. It will be possible to spend so much time developing the infinitely perfect **'Grand Plan'** that you cannot implement it because it is too late to achieve your objectives.

- You will need to lead your people and manage your things in a way that is focused on achieving your defined objectives. You should not reorganize for the sake of reorganizing. Routines and processes that are not broken do not need to be repaired. You should remain mindful that you are a small unit leader. Accomplishing your objectives will contribute to your organization's overall strategy and goals.

- You will direct your people's activities using your common sense communications skills as discussed above. You will also need to be attentive to the things you manage in order to ensure they are available and ready to use when your people need them.

- You will continually monitor and control your unit's activities to ensure that progress is being made as planned. You will need to correct situations that are not focused on achieving the desired results.

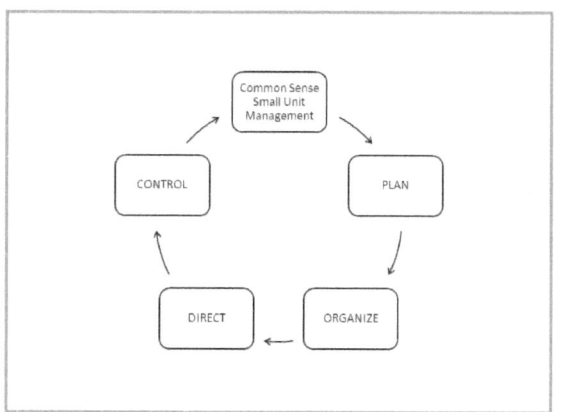

Figure 3 Management Cycle

"Management is doing things right. Leadership is doing the right things"

Peter Drucker (1909 – 2005)

In summary, you will need to balance effectiveness and efficiency, **favoring effectiveness**. Effectiveness will relate to doing the things that contribute to your objectives while efficiency will relate to doing whatever it is you do while consuming the minimum amount of resources possible. For example, a team could rob a bank very efficiently, but would robbing a bank really be the right thing to do?

As a small unit leader you will be in a position to directly lead people and manage things so as to be sure that your collective efforts are directed toward accomplishing legitimate results in the form of achieving your planned objectives. You should monitor the consumption of resources to enhance your unit's efficiency, but not at the expense of effectiveness.

Chapter Five

Where to lead?

"Go where the action is."

General of the Army Omar Bradley (1897 – 1981)

You will need to place yourself wherever you will best be able to contribute to the success of the endeavor at hand. Leadership from the front has been a long standing concept but the passage of time and the advancement of technology have re-defined where the front is located. You will need to be where you can best lead, communicate and allocate resources in support of your team's activities. You should be accessing whatever network, system and infrastructure you need to lead your people and manage your things.

Direct, close-up leadership has not always been the actual practice of military leaders. For centuries, the general officers of Western Europe achieved their rank and positions by virtue of family connections and/or personal wealth. Examples abound of British colonial military campaigns that were led by senior officers who transported their luxurious households to remote, foreign locations such as the Crimea and Sub-Saharan Africa. These Generals (royalty or not) led from great distances and through layers of intermediaries. Timely decisions and adroit adjustments to tactical situations simply did not occur. The infamous and disastrous *'Charge of the Light Brigade'* during the Crimean War in the middle of the nineteenth century was a deadly blunder that resulted from garbled and unclear commands received by a brave but doomed cavalry unit.

In 1979, I had the great privilege to attend a luncheon at White Sands Missile Range, New Mexico where the Guest of Honor was General of the Army (GOA) Omar Bradley. General of the Army and Mrs. Bradley were then living in nearby Ft Bliss, Texas, near El Paso. The General's advanced age excused him from making any lengthy speeches, but he did offer to answer a few questions from the attendees after lunch.

I recall only two of the questions and his answers. One was the funniest question. It was asked by a Navy Captain. He asked the general if he had decided yet if he was going to make the military a career. In fact, GOA Bradley's service began in 1911 when he entered West Point. On the day of the luncheon in 1979, the general had about 68 years invested in one of the most honorable military careers before or since. However, GOA Bradley chuckled and casually responded that he "was still thinking about it."

The other question I remember was more serious and more meaningful. General of the Army Bradley was asked what singular piece of advice he would give to the aspiring young leaders who were gathered around him at the luncheon.

His response was as succinct as it was valuable. He simply said: "**Go where the action is.**" A number of historians have written about General Bradley's actions in the European Theatre of Operations (ETO) during World War II. In November of 1943 he precipitated the surrender of 250,000 Axis troops near Bizerte, Tunisia. At the time he was serving as a subordinate of Lieutenant General George S Patton. Only a year later, in 1944, he had been promoted to be General Patton's superior during the drive across France and into Germany to end the war.

General Bradley's nickname among the soldiers in his units was "The G.I. General". He got this moniker by moving around within and among the frontline fighting units. He shared tents, meals and transport with the lowest enlisted ranks on many occasions. He even shared their transport when that transport was a pair of muddy boots.

Some years after the luncheon where GOA Bradley had shared his advice, I was assigned as the leader of a small unit that operated and maintained a large computer system and associated terminal network. It was at an early point along the timeline of what we now call the Internet. Moore's Law about the shrinking size of computer equipment compared to its processing power had not yet taken effect.

Immediately upon taking responsibility for operation of the networked computer system, I realized that the network was the more challenging part. An entire wall of the raised floor computer room contained a network hub for over a hundred data links. Some of the links were 100 feet away; some were 2 miles away; while some were 1500 miles away. These links soon became the center and the bane of my existence.

On one occasion, I was attempting to discern why one of the nearby links was dropping its connection. I decided to take GOA Bradley's advice from that luncheon a long time ago. I walked to the room where the corresponding network node was located. That node supported a cluster of end users who accessed the services of the computer system.

I discovered at the end user node that a secretary had followed her boss's direction and obtained a new coffee pot to provide handier, fresher coffee for the boss and others in the office. She placed the new coffee pot into use by plugging it into the power outlet where our end user node had been plugged. The end user node was not communicating with the hub in the computer room because it had been unplugged from its power source. I explained the situation to the boss and offered to provide an inexpensive power strip so that both the network node and the coffee pot could both be plugged in at the same time. He agreed and the problem was resolved.

General of the Army Bradley was right. His action was in a combat zone. Mine was in an air conditioned office environment. My easy and convenient stroll to the end user location resolved a communication failure quickly, easily and inexpensively. I began making regular visits to all the end user nodes. Many could be visited by walking down the hall. Others required getting into a car. Yet others involved airplanes.

It didn't matter. I went where the action was and increased the reliability and quality of network access for thousands of end users. I passed this practice on to my successors in that position as what became known as 'Walking the Perimeter'.

In 1985, Tom Peters and Robert Waterman wrote a book called *A Passion for Excellence – The Leadership Difference*. One of the excellent practices they cited in successful companies of the time was 'Management by Wandering Around'. They emphasized that the leader who wanders around maximizes their time spent moving around if they actively get in touch with the people they wander among. For example, leaders of sales units need to be in touch with both customers and sales people.

Peters and Waterman described an instance of major commercial failure when the wandering around was not done with enough forethought. All General Motors executives in the late seventies and eighties drove GM cars, by definition. The executives in Detroit often travelled throughout the mid-west and east coast regions of the US. During these travels they carefully observed that most other cars they saw on the road and in hotel garages, etc. were American, if not GM. They knew that the GM cars they drove performed very well and were well maintained.

Unfortunately, the executives hardly ever travelled to California where many American consumers were recognizing the values in fuel economy and reliability of Asian automobiles. The insular executives were soon overwhelmed by imported cars that they failed to notice while wandering in a limited way while wearing blinders.

A more encouraging example that Peters and Waterman found was a medical equipment manufacturing firm. All unit leaders in the firm were required to phone a customer who had purchased a piece of their equipment each week. Their conversation was scripted to start with one very sensible question: "What is your level of satisfaction with the equipment and the way it is operating for you?"

A widely read commercial business text such as this identified what is basically an equivalent idea to GOA Bradley's "**Go where the action is**". While GOA Bradley's action was in combat, the commercial business leader's action is in a routine work environment. The work may be designing an item, producing an item, selling an item, warehousing an item, servicing an item, transporting it or disposing of it. The work may be preparing and serving good, healthy food, or replacing the tires on a car. In any case, effective small unit leaders go directly to the place where they can best support that work. That place may be close enough to taste the food or it may be thousands of miles away at a place where a critical support item needs to be expedited at its point of origin.

The choice of the right place must be driven by a common sense assessment of the situation at the time.

Chapter Six

When to lead?

"Earn your leadership every day."

Michael Jordan

Leadership, like money, has time value. You need to be ready to lead at any time.

There will be a time to assert leadership and a time to go with the flow. Your people will become the professionals that you have enabled them to be. You will need to be able to maintain situational awareness of your unit's activities and progress toward your objectives without interfering in the work itself.

Successful leaders will have motivated their people in such a way that people know what to do and why, even in the leader's absence. Your people will not need to be reminded constantly of how, when or where to do what needs to be done. They will know who needs to do what and when. In short, they will be self-motivated and self-reliant.

Only when they need guidance should you give it. You should manage the unit's resources so that all of the things that they require will be available when and where they are needed.

You should also be attentive to the time that you and your people actually spend in pursuit of the unit's objectives. A balance of work/family/pleasure will be required.   The needs of your people will include time for their basic human needs and the more advanced social needs as well.

You will need to be generous with your time and your leadership. You will be a better leader if you are willing to listen to personal issues at work, at home, or in a social setting. You will guide your people best by your own example. One great example to set will be to always be attentive to ideas, thoughts, problems and feelings.

Afterword

Early in their book entitled *Team of Teams*, General Stan McChrystal, et al, pointed to the famous naval Battle of Trafalgar that took place in 1805. In that battle, British Admiral Nelson defeated a much larger combined Spanish and French armada. He did so by employing an unorthodox attack. It was unorthodox because it was based on Admiral Nelson decomposing his fleet into a number of individual small units (ships in his case) that attacked and fought the Spanish and French fleet in direct single-ship match-ups.

Nelson's success was an aggregate of small unit successes carried out by individual ship Captains. The 'micro-level' unit victories accumulated into an overall victory of the smaller British fleet over the larger Spanish and French armada.

You should now be more ready to be an effective small unit leader in your environment, whatever it is. You will lead your people and manage your things so as to be successful in contributing to a higher level of success for your organization. That organization might be a large corporation that provides retail products to a vast clientele. That organization might be a small company that provides a service to a local community in your area. That organization might be a volunteer fire department that is keeping your fellow citizens safe.

You will lead one of those small, focused teams that are better able to be adaptive and flexible in their efforts to be effective in contributing to our society.

There are no war stories in this book. It is axiomatic that the epitome of small unit leadership is leadership in mortal combat. There is an excellent contemporary book on this subject titled *The Leader's Code* by Captain Donovan Campbell (Random House, New York, 2013). I recommend it.

References / Resources

Atkinson, Rick, *An Army at Dawn*, New York, Henry Holt and Company, 2002

Ballard, Greg, *Small Unit Leadership*, Bloomington, In, Author House, 2005

Campbell, Donovan, *The Leader's Code*, New York, Random House, 2013.

Drucker, Peter F., *The Effective Executive*, New York, Harper Collins Inc., 2002

Edinger, Edward F. MD, "*An Outline of Analytical Psychology*", New York, The Quadrant, Jung Foundation for Analytical Psychology, 1968

Giles, Lionel, *Sun Tsu on the Art of War*, London, The British Museum Press, 1910

Jacobi, Jolande, *The Psychology of C G Jung*, New Haven, Yale University Press, 1943

Malone, Dandridge M., *Small Unit Leadership – A Commonsense Approach*, Novato, CA, Presidio Press, 1983

Maslow, A.H., *"A Theory of Human Motivation"*, Washington, DC, Psychological Review, Vol 50, 1943

McChrystal, Stan, et al, *Team of Teams*, New York, Penguin Random House LLC, 2015

Northouse, Peter G., *Introduction to Leadership – Concepts and Practice*, Los Angeles, Sage Publications Inc., 2009

Peters, Tom, et al, *A Passion for Excellence – The Leadership Difference*, New York, Warner Books, 1985

U.S. Army, *Field Manual 6-22 – Leadership*, Stilwell, KS, Digireads Publications Inc., 2007

www.brainyquote.com

www.dictionary.com

www.Forbes.com

www.myersbriggs.org

www.va.gov

www.wikipedia.org

Appendix A
The Un-Leader

The un-leader has two primary motivators: **greed and fear**.

Their **greed** causes every word and deed to be oriented on gaining the greatest benefit for themselves, in the moment. They care not about the team, the organization or anyone else. They prefer the pronoun '**I**' to '**we**'. They do not believe in the concept of mutual respect. All respect and loyalty is due them. They owe neither respect nor loyalty to anyone. The result of this is that the un-leader is not able to recognize win-win situations when they present themselves. The un-leader knows in their gut that they can only win if someone else loses, dramatically.   They simply cannot function as team players.

Their **fear** makes them overreact to any criticism by denying everything, admitting nothing and counter accusing someone else without regard to the truth of the matter.   They frequently act out of exaggerated fear that is exacerbated by frequent mood shifts. They are unable to engage in rational, balanced analysis of situations and problems. Instead, their decisions and directions are erratic, reflexive and obsessive. Hate and spite can often be seen in their very poor decisions.

They routinely speak to people in a way that makes it clear that they see their own ego as their audience rather than the team or the group. It is a time tested adage that "An honorable person's word is their bond." The un-leader honors their word only by accident.

Gordon Gekko was wrong. Greed is not good – especially when it shows up as a principal motivator for someone who pretends to be a leader.

Franklin Delano Roosevelt was right. "The only thing we have to fear is fear itself "– especially when it shows up as the other principal motivator for a would-be leader.

Beware these un-leaders. They exist in every organization, small and large. The larger the organization the more un-leaders there are. You may find yourself answering to someone who is less of a leader than you are.

Small unit un-leaders are conspicuous by the way they tend to refer to themselves. They consistently label themselves as 'managers'. They are not your leader, they are your manager.

The manager will always emphasize that it is you who have the responsibility to create success or failure for yourself and your team, not them. They will loudly cheer you on and hand you objectives and goals. They will provide things that might help you create success that will accrue primarily to them.

The manager will overwhelm you with motivators. These motivators will be largely in the form of money or other material enticements. You will be reminded daily that you can get luxury trips, decadent jewelry, cash, gift cards, etc. These are the things that motivate them, so they think they will do the same for you.

Frequently, the performance of the people in the unit determines the personal compensation of the manager. The more the people in the unit generate in revenue, the more the managers earn for themselves. The managers satisfy their **greed** by appealing to yours.

The managers also live in constant **fear** that they will be judged harshly by their superior managers in the larger organization above them. The higher level managers create and manipulate the established objectives, goals and metrics on a constant basis so as to keep the subordinate managers jumping.

I have watched a unit manager physically twitch and convulse while that manager was nervously ranting about the latest change in incentive packages to spur greater production on the part of his unit's workers. This manager's obvious nervousness was rooted in the manager's constant fear of being judged as under producing or slow to adopt new guidance.

The result of his series of constant knee jerk reactions was a disjointed and confused approach to the actual work at hand. This, ironically, ended up diminishing production rather than enhancing it.

Production process changes need time to demonstrate their effectiveness. Their efficiency also needs to be gauged over a reasonable period of time. Constant, reflexive changes will be counter-productive in most environments.

This observation does not contain personal descriptions of any living person(s).

Appendix B

Summary of the Psychology of C. G. Jung

Carl Gustav Jung was born on 26 July 1875 in Switzerland. Jung studied medicine in Basel but began his career in psychiatry in Zürich in 1900. Jung had a period of close collaboration with Sigmund Freud starting around 1907. Jung intensely studied Freud's theories of psychoanalysis. In 1909 Jung left academia to work as a physician and a psychotherapist. He also conducted scientific research and wrote extensively. In 1911 Jung founded and became the first President of the International Psychoanalytic Association which included Freud as a member.

In 1912 Jung published a research paper concerning his interpretation of the human libido which was critical of Freud's thoughts and ideas. Jung departed from Freud's school of thought and pursued his own extensive research into the nature of the individual human unconscious. Jung also delved deeply into what he called the collective unconscious and how it related to the individual.

Jung's research involved spending time in North Africa and the Southwest United States studying the Pueblo Indian tribe. He also studied African tribal norms in Kenya and delved into Oriental symbols and philosophies including that of Taoism. Jung also explored various cultural mythologies in his pursuit of a better understanding of his concept of the collective unconscious.

During the 1930's Jung served as the head of several societies for the advancement of psychotherapy. In 1936 Harvard University declared him one of the outstanding living scientists and conferred upon him an honorary degree. Jung's works have been translated into almost all European and some non-European language. In 1961 Jung died after a short illness.

The C. G. Young Institute was formed in 1948 to support the pursuit of advancing Jung's ideas and the work of other prominent scientists. It has advanced training and research in analytic psychology. Its founding staff was made up of highly experienced specialists trained by Jung himself. Students of the Institute still undergo an analysis of about 300 sessions and conduct supervised analyses totaling at least 250 hours in order to obtain the institute's coveted diploma.

The biographical sketch above is drawn from *The Psychology of C G Jung*, written in 1943 by a protégé of Jung named Dr. Jolande Jacobi. Dr. Jacobi wrote the book with the support and collaboration of Dr. Jung himself. Dr. Jung penned an introduction to the book in which he explained that he had never found the time to do a proper and clear summary of his basic ideas, concepts and theories. He was grateful that Dr. Jacobi had done so and he endorsed her work as full, complete and accurate.

Dr. Jung's concept of Analytical Psychology was, in fact, more expansive and inclusive than those of Sigmund Freud or Alfred Adler. Dr. Jung attributed great influence to what he called primordial instincts that are represented in a shared, collective unconscious in addition to the classically defined individual unconscious.

Recent advances in the science of human genome mapping have provided some credence to Jung's postulation about the collective unconscious as a reflection of those primordial, tribal influences that come to people through their heredity.

Dr. Jung's definition of the Libido differed from others in that he saw it as the energy used by an individual to choose between a set of innate diametrically opposed preferences with which all people are born. He saw it as a more neutral entity than was widely accepted at the outset of the study of human psychology.

Dr. Jung saw a set of innately different psychological types that might define a person's psyche. These types are based upon a person's natural preferences or choices between multiple ways of responding to the world, including:

- There is a choice between introversion and extraversion.
- There is a choice between thinking and feeling.
- There is a choice between sensing and intuiting.
- There is a choice between judging and sensing.

Some of his earliest work included word association tests which measured the extent to which any given person might be inclined to choose among the these opposites.

Appendix C
A summary of my Myers - Briggs Type Inventory

Personality type is a practical framework for understanding differences among people. According to the results of my own MBTI testing, I am characterized as an **"ISTJ"** from among the 16 possible types below. This signifies that my personality type is one that is **I**ntroverted, **S**ensing, **T**hinking and **J**udging.

ISTJ	ISFJ	INFJ	INTJ
Responsible Executors	Dedicated Stewards	Insightful Motivators	Visionary Strategists
ISTP	**ISFP**	**INFP**	**INTP**
Nimble Pragmatics	Practical Custodians	Inspired Crusaders	Expansive Analyzers
ESTP	**ESFP**	**ENFP**	**ENTP**
Dynamic Mavericks	Enthusiastic Improvisors	Impassioned Catalysts	Innovative Explorers
ESTJ	**ESFJ**	**ENFJ**	**ENTJ**
Efficient Drivers	Committed Builders	Engaging Mobilizers	Strategic Directors

We ISTJs are quiet, serious people who succeed by being thorough and dependable. We are logical, practical, and realistic. We take our work seriously and often go beyond the call of duty. We enjoy ordering and structuring our environment and our work. Traditions and loyalty are also important to us.

We represent approximately 12 percent of the US population.

We share the following characteristics:

- We are mainly interested in the realities we perceive with our five senses.

- We know what has worked in the past and base our decisions on facts and experience.

- We value security and stability.

- We take a logical, analytical approach to problems.

- We tend to put off play or leisure until all our responsibilities are met.

We tend to interact with others in the following ways:

- We have a strong sense of loyalty and responsibility to our families and relationships.

- We share our humor and our many rich observations/memories only with close friends.

- We sometimes try to help others by pointing out what they are doing wrong.

- We tend to express our caring through actions rather than words.

- We always follow through on our commitments to others.

- We may have difficulty making sense of needs that differ widely from our own.

We approach work in the following ways:

- We prefer to focus on the task rather than on the people involved.

- We work to establish standard policies and procedures.

- Our motto is usually: "If it ain't broke, don't fix it."

- We will support change only when convinced it will bring better results.

- We are logical and analytical, readily spotting the flaws in ideas and immediately pointing out why something won't work.

- When we see that something needs to be done, we accept the responsibility, often going beyond the call of duty.

- We often choose careers in which we are less likely to be happy in work that demands mastery of abstract ideas or that requires constant and close contact with people.

We need to be attentive to the following potential limitations:

- If we have not developed our Sensing preference, we may not take in enough facts and then may rush into action prematurely.

- If we don't take in enough information, we run the risk of passing judgment on others inappropriately.

- We may be suspicious of imagination and intuition, and may not take them seriously.

- We may expect everyone to be as logical and analytical as we are and become impatient when events prove otherwise.

- If we have not developed our Thinking preference, we may retreat from the world, becoming absorbed with our inner reactions and impressions, and produce little of value.

- If we have not developed our Feeling preference, we can sometimes appear critical of others.

Appendix D

A Theory of Human Motivation

A. H. Maslow (1943)

Originally Published in *Psychological Review*, 50, 370-396.

[p. 370] I. INTRODUCTION

In a previous paper (13) various propositions were presented which would have to be included in any theory of human motivation that could lay claim to being definitive. These conclusions may be briefly summarized as follows:

1. The integrated wholeness of the organism must be one of the foundation stones of motivation theory.

2. The hunger drive (or any other physiological drive) was rejected as a centering point or model for a definitive theory of motivation. Any drive that is somatically based and localizable was shown to be atypical rather than typical in human motivation.

3. Such a theory should stress and center itself upon ultimate or basic goals rather than partial or superficial ones, upon ends rather than means to these ends. Such a stress would imply a more central place for unconscious than for conscious motivations.

4. There are usually available various cultural paths to the same goal. Therefore conscious, specific, local-cultural desires are not as fundamental in motivation theory as the more basic, unconscious goals.

5. Any motivated behavior, either preparatory or consummatory, must be understood to be a channel through which many basic needs may be simultaneously expressed or satisfied. Typically an act has more than one motivation.

6. Practically all organismic states are to be understood as motivated and as motivating.

7. Human needs arrange themselves in hierarchies of pre-potency. That is to say, the appearance of one need usually rests on the prior satisfaction of another, more pre-potent need. Man is a perpetually wanting animal. Also no need or drive can be treated as if it were isolated or discrete; every drive is related to the state of satisfaction or dissatisfaction of other drives.

8. *Lists* of drives will get us nowhere for various theoretical and practical reasons. Furthermore any classification of motivations [p. 371] must deal with the problem of levels of specificity or generalization the motives to be classified.

9. Classifications of motivations must be based upon goals rather than upon instigating drives or motivated behavior.

10. Motivation theory should be human-centered rather than animal-centered.

11. The situation or the field in which the organism reacts must be taken into account but the field alone can rarely serve as an exclusive explanation for behavior. Furthermore the field itself must be interpreted in terms of the organism. Field theory cannot be a substitute for motivation theory.

12. Not only the integration of the organism must be taken into account, but also the possibility of isolated, specific, partial or segmental reactions. It has since become necessary to add to these another affirmation.

13. Motivation theory is not synonymous with behavior theory. The motivations are only one class of determinants of behavior. While behavior is almost always motivated, it is also almost always biologically, culturally and situationally determined as well.

The present paper is an attempt to formulate a positive theory of motivation which will satisfy these theoretical demands and at the same time conform to the known facts, clinical and observational as well as experimental. It derives most directly, however, from clinical experience. This theory is, I think, in the functionalist tradition of James and Dewey, and is fused with the holism of Wertheimer (19), Goldstein (6), and Gestalt Psychology, and with the dynamicism of Freud (4) and Adler (1). This fusion or synthesis may arbitrarily be called a 'general-dynamic' theory.

It is far easier to perceive and to criticize the aspects in motivation theory than to remedy them. Mostly this is because of the very serious lack of sound data in this area. I conceive this lack of sound facts to be due primarily to the absence of a valid theory of motivation. The present theory then must be considered to be a suggested program or framework for future research and must stand or fall, not so much on facts available or evidence presented, as upon researches to be done, researches suggested perhaps, by the questions raised in this paper.[p. 372]

II. THE BASIC NEEDS

The 'physiological' needs. -- The needs that are usually taken as the starting point for motivation theory are the so-called physiological drives. Two recent lines of research make it necessary to revise our customary notions about these needs, first, the development of the concept of homeostasis, and second, the finding that appetites (preferential choices among foods) are a fairly efficient indication of actual needs or lacks in the body.

Homeostasis refers to the body's automatic efforts to maintain a constant, normal state of the blood stream. Cannon (2) has described this process for (1) the water content of the blood, (2) salt content, (3) sugar content, (4) protein content, (5) fat content, (6) calcium content, (7) oxygen content, (8) constant hydrogen-ion level (acid-base balance) and (9) constant temperature of the blood. Obviously this list can be extended to include other minerals, the hormones, vitamins, etc.

Young in a recent article (21) has summarized the work on appetite in its relation to body needs. If the body lacks some chemical, the individual will tend to develop a specific appetite or partial hunger for that food element.

Thus it seems impossible as well as useless to make any list of fundamental physiological needs for they can come to almost any number one might wish, depending on the degree of specificity of description. We cannot identify all physiological needs as homeostatic. That sexual desire, sleepiness, sheer activity and maternal behavior in animals, are homeostatic, has not yet been demonstrated. Furthermore, this list would not include the various sensory pleasures (tastes, smells, tickling, stroking) which are probably physiological and which may become the goals of motivated behavior.

In a previous paper (13) it has been pointed out that these physiological drives or needs are to be considered unusual rather than typical because they are isolable, and because they are localizable somatically. That is to say, they are relatively independent of each other, of other motivations [p. 373] and of the organism as a whole, and secondly, in many cases, it is possible to demonstrate a localized, underlying somatic base for the drive. This is true less generally than has been thought (exceptions are fatigue, sleepiness, and maternal responses) but it is still true in the classic instances of hunger, sex, and thirst.

It should be pointed out again that any of the physiological needs and the consummatory behavior involved with them serve as channels for all sorts of other needs as well. That is to say, the person who thinks he is hungry may actually be seeking more for comfort, or dependence, than for vitamins or proteins. Conversely, it is possible to satisfy the hunger need in part by other activities such as drinking water or smoking cigarettes. In other words, relatively isolable as these physiological needs are, they are not completely so.

Undoubtedly these physiological needs are the most pre-potent of all needs. What this means specifically is, that in the human being who is missing everything in life in an extreme fashion, it is most likely that the major motivation would be the physiological needs rather than any others. A person who is lacking food, safety, love, and esteem would most probably hunger for food more strongly than for anything else.

If all the needs are unsatisfied, and the organism is then dominated by the physiological needs, all other needs may become simply non-existent or be pushed into the background. It is then fair to characterize the whole organism by saying simply that it is hungry, for consciousness is almost completely preempted by hunger. All capacities are put into the service of hunger-satisfaction, and the organization of these capacities is almost entirely determined by the one purpose of satisfying hunger. The receptors and effectors, the intelligence, memory, habits, all may now be defined simply as hunger-gratifying tools. Capacities that are not useful for this purpose lie dormant, or are pushed into the background. The urge to write poetry, the desire to acquire an automobile, the interest in American history, the desire for a new pair of shoes are, in the extreme case, forgotten or become of secondary -[p.374] importance. For the man who is extremely and dangerously hungry, no other interests exist but food. He dreams food, he remembers food, he thinks about food, he emotes only about food, he perceives only food and he wants only food. The more subtle determinants that ordinarily fuse with the physiological drives in organizing even feeding, drinking or sexual behavior, may now be so completely overwhelmed as to allow us to speak at this time (but only at this time) of pure hunger drive and behavior, with the one unqualified aim of relief.

Another peculiar characteristic of the human organism when it is dominated by a certain need is that the whole philosophy of the future tends also to change. For our chronically and extremely hungry man, Utopia can be defined very simply as a place where there is plenty of food. He tends to think that, if only he is guaranteed food for the rest of his life, he will be perfectly happy and will never want anything more. Life itself tends to be defined in terms of eating. Anything else will be defined as unimportant. Freedom, love, community feeling, respect, philosophy, may all be waved aside as fripperies which are useless since they fail to fill the stomach. Such a man may fairly be said to live by bread alone.

It cannot possibly be denied that such things are true but their *generality* can be denied. Emergency conditions are, almost by definition, rare in the normally functioning peaceful society. That this truism can be forgotten is due mainly to two reasons. First, rats have few motivations other than physiological ones, and since so much of the research upon motivation has been made with these animals, it is easy to carry the rat-picture over to the human being. Secondly, it is too often not realized that culture itself is an adaptive tool, one of whose main functions is to make the physiological emergencies come less and less often. In most of the known societies, chronic extreme hunger of the emergency type is rare, rather than common. In any case, this is still true in the United States. The average American citizen is experiencing appetite rather than hunger when he says "I am [p. 375] hungry." He is apt to experience sheer life-and-death hunger only by accident and then only a few times through his entire life.

Obviously a good way to obscure the 'higher' motivations, and to get a lopsided view of human capacities and human nature, is to make the organism extremely and chronically hungry or thirsty. Anyone who attempts to make an emergency picture into a typical one, and who will measure all of man's goals and desires by his behavior during extreme physiological deprivation is certainly being blind to many things. It is quite true that man lives by bread alone -- when there is no bread. But what happens to man's desires when there is plenty of bread and when his belly is chronically filled?

At once other (and 'higher') needs emerge and these, rather than physiological hungers, dominate the organism. And when these in turn are satisfied, again new (and still 'higher') needs emerge and so on. This is what we mean by saying that the basic human needs are organized into a hierarchy of relative prepotency.

One main implication of this phrasing is that gratification becomes as important a concept as deprivation in motivation theory, for it releases the organism from the domination of a relatively more physiological need, permitting thereby the emergence of other more social goals. The physiological needs, along with their partial goals, when chronically gratified cease to exist as active determinants or organizers of behavior. They now exist only in a potential fashion in the sense that they may emerge again to dominate the organism if they are thwarted. But a want that is satisfied is no longer a want. The organism is dominated and its behavior organized only by unsatisfied needs. If hunger is satisfied, it becomes unimportant in the current dynamics of the individual.

This statement is somewhat qualified by a hypothesis to be discussed more fully later, namely that it is precisely those individuals in whom a certain need has always been satisfied who are best equipped to tolerate deprivation of that need in the future, and that furthermore, those who have been deprived -[p. 376] in the past will react differently to current satisfactions than the one who has never been deprived.

The safety needs. -- If the physiological needs are relatively well gratified, there then emerges a new set of needs, which we may categorize roughly as the safety needs. All that has been said of the physiological needs is equally true, although in lesser degree, of these desires. The organism may equally well be wholly dominated by them. They may serve as the almost exclusive organizers of behavior, recruiting all the capacities of the organism in their service, and we may then fairly describe the whole organism as a safety-seeking mechanism. Again we may say of the receptors, the effectors, of the intellect and the other capacities that they are primarily safety-seeking tools. Again, as in the hungry man, we find that the dominating goal is a strong determinant not only of his current world-outlook and philosophy but also of his philosophy of the future. Practically everything looks less important than safety, (even sometimes the physiological needs which being satisfied, are now underestimated). A man, in this state, if it is extreme enough and chronic enough, may be characterized as living almost for safety alone.

Although in this paper we are interested primarily in the needs of the adult, we can approach an understanding of his safety needs perhaps more efficiently by observation of infants and children, in whom these needs are much more simple and obvious. One reason for the clearer appearance of the threat or danger reaction in infants, is that they do not inhibit this reaction at all, whereas adults in our society have been taught to inhibit it at all costs. Thus even when adults do feel their safety to be threatened we may not be able to see this on the surface. Infants will react in a total fashion and as if they were endangered, if they are disturbed or dropped suddenly, startled by loud noises, flashing light, or other unusual sensory stimulation, by rough handling, by general loss of support in the mother's arms, or by inadequate support.[1][p. 377]

In infants we can also see a much more direct reaction to bodily illnesses of various kinds. Sometimes these illnesses seem to be immediately and *per se* threatening and seem to make the child feel unsafe. For instance, vomiting, colic or other sharp pains seem to make the child look at the whole world in a different way. At such a moment of pain, it may be postulated that, for the child, the appearance of the whole world suddenly changes from sunniness to darkness, so to speak, and becomes a place in which anything at all might happen, in which previously stable things have suddenly become unstable. Thus a child who because of some bad food is taken ill may, for a day or two, develop fear, nightmares, and a need for protection and reassurance never seen in him before his illness.

Another indication of the child's need for safety is his preference for some kind of undisrupted routine or rhythm. He seems to want a predictable, orderly world. For instance, injustice, unfairness, or inconsistency in the parents seems to make a child feel anxious and unsafe. This attitude may be not so much because of the injustice *per se* or any particular pains involved, but rather because this treatment threatens to make the world look unreliable, or unsafe, or unpredictable. Young children seem to thrive better under a system which has at least a skeletal outline of rigidity, in which there is a schedule of a kind, some sort of routine, something that can be counted upon, not only for the present but also far into the future. Perhaps one could express this more accurately by saying that the child needs an organized world rather than an unorganized or unstructured one.

The central role of the parents and the normal family setup are indisputable. Quarreling, physical assault, separation, divorce or death within the family may be particularly terrifying. Also parental outbursts of rage or threats of punishment directed to the child, calling him names, speaking to him harshly, shaking him, handling him roughly, or actual [p. 378] physical punishment sometimes elicit such total panic and terror in the child that we must assume more is involved than the physical pain alone. While it is true that in some children this terror may represent also a fear of loss of parental love, it can also occur in completely rejected children, who seem to cling to the hating parents more for sheer safety and protection than because of hope of love.

Confronting the average child with new, unfamiliar, strange, unmanageable stimuli or situations will too frequently elicit the danger or terror reaction, as for example, getting lost or even being separated from the parents for a short time, being confronted with new faces, new situations or new tasks, the sight of strange, unfamiliar or uncontrollable objects, illness or death. Particularly at such times, the child's frantic clinging to his parents is eloquent testimony to their role as protectors (quite apart from their roles as food-givers and love-givers).

From these and similar observations, we may generalize and say that the average child in our society generally prefers a safe, orderly, predictable, organized world, which he can count, on, and in which unexpected, unmanageable or other dangerous things do not happen, and in which, in any case, he has all-powerful parents who protect and shield him from harm.

That these reactions may so easily be observed in children is in a way a proof of the fact that children in our society, feel too unsafe (or, in a word, are badly brought up). Children who are reared in an unthreatening, loving family do not ordinarily react as we have described above (17). In such children the danger reactions are apt to come mostly to objects or situations that adults too would consider dangerous.[2]

The healthy, normal, fortunate adult in our culture is largely satisfied in his safety needs. The peaceful, smoothly [p. 379] running, 'good' society ordinarily makes its members feel safe enough from wild animals, extremes of temperature, criminals, assault and murder, tyranny, etc. Therefore, in a very real sense, he no longer has any safety needs as active motivators. Just as a sated man no longer feels hungry, a safe man no longer feels endangered. If we wish to see these needs directly and clearly we must turn to neurotic or near-neurotic individuals, and to the economic and social underdogs. In between these extremes, we can perceive the expressions of safety needs only in such phenomena as, for instance, the common preference for a job with tenure and protection, the desire for a savings account, and for insurance of various kinds (medical, dental, unemployment, disability, old age).

Other broader aspects of the attempt to seek safety and stability in the world are seen in the very common preference for familiar rather than unfamiliar things, or for the known rather than the unknown. The tendency to have some religion or world-philosophy that organizes the universe and the men in it into some sort of satisfactorily coherent, meaningful whole is also in part motivated by safety-seeking. Here too we may list science and philosophy in general as partially motivated by the safety needs (we shall see later that there are also other motivations to scientific, philosophical or religious endeavor).

Otherwise the need for safety is seen as an active and dominant mobilizer of the organism's resources only in emergencies, *e. g.*, war, disease, natural catastrophes, crime waves, societal disorganization, neurosis, brain injury, chronically bad situation.

Some neurotic adults in our society are, in many ways, like the unsafe child in their desire for safety, although in the former it takes on a somewhat special appearance. Their reaction is often to unknown, psychological dangers in a world that is perceived to be hostile, overwhelming and threatening. Such a person behaves as if a great catastrophe were almost always impending, i.e., he is usually responding as if to an emergency. His safety needs often find specific [p. 380] expression in a search for a protector, or a stronger person on whom he may depend, or perhaps, a Fuehrer.

The neurotic individual may be described in a slightly different way with some usefulness as a grown-up person who retains his childish attitudes toward the world. That is to say, a neurotic adult may be said to behave 'as if' he were actually afraid of a spanking, or of his mother's disapproval, or of being abandoned by his parents, or having his food taken away from him. It is as if his childish attitudes of fear and threat reaction to a dangerous world had gone underground, and untouched by the growing up and learning processes, were now ready to be called out by any stimulus that would make a child feel endangered and threatened.[3]

The neurosis in which the search for safety takes its dearest form is in the compulsive-obsessive neurosis. Compulsive-obsessives try frantically to order and stabilize the world so that no unmanageable, unexpected or unfamiliar dangers will ever appear (14); They hedge themselves about with all sorts of ceremonials, rules and formulas so that every possible contingency may be provided for and so that no new contingencies may appear. They are much like the brain injured cases, described by Goldstein (6), who manage to maintain their equilibrium by avoiding everything unfamiliar and strange and by ordering their restricted world in such a neat, disciplined, orderly fashion that everything in the world can be counted upon. They try to arrange the world so that anything unexpected (dangers) cannot possibly occur. If, through no fault of their own, something unexpected does occur, they go into a panic reaction as if this unexpected occurrence constituted a grave danger. What we can see only as a none-too-strong preference in the healthy person, *e. g.*, preference for the familiar, becomes a life-and-death. necessity in abnormal cases.

The love needs. -- If both the physiological and the safety needs are fairly well gratified, then there will emerge the love and affection and belongingness needs, and the whole cycle [p. 381] already described will repeat itself with this new center. Now the person will feel keenly, as never before, the absence of friends, or a sweetheart, or a wife, or children. He will hunger for affectionate relations with people in general, namely, for a place in his group, and he will strive with great intensity to achieve this goal. He will want to attain such a place more than anything else in the world and may even forget that once, when he was hungry, he sneered at love.

In our society the thwarting of these needs is the most commonly found core in cases of maladjustment and more severe psychopathology. Love and affection, as well as their possible expression in sexuality, are generally looked upon with ambivalence and are customarily hedged about with many restrictions and inhibitions. Practically all theorists of psychopathology have stressed thwarting of the love needs as basic in the picture of maladjustment. Many clinical studies have therefore been made of this need and we know more about it perhaps than any of the other needs except the physiological ones (14).

One thing that must be stressed at this point is that love is not synonymous with sex. Sex may be studied as a purely physiological need. Ordinarily sexual behavior is multi-determined, that is to say, determined not only by sexual but also by other needs, chief among which are the love and affection needs. Also not to be overlooked is the fact that the love needs involve both giving *and* receiving love.[4]

The esteem needs. -- All people in our society (with a few pathological exceptions) have a need or desire for a stable, firmly based, (usually) high evaluation of themselves, for self-respect, or self-esteem, and for the esteem of others. By firmly based self-esteem, we mean that which is soundly based upon real capacity, achievement and respect from others. These needs may be classified into two subsidiary sets. These are, first, the desire for strength, for achievement, for adequacy, for confidence in the face of the world, and for independence and freedom.[5] Secondly, we have what [p. 382] we may call the desire for reputation or prestige (defining it as respect or esteem from other people), recognition, attention, importance or appreciation.[6] These needs have been relatively stressed by Alfred Adler and his followers, and have been relatively neglected by Freud and the psychoanalysts. More and more today however there is appearing widespread appreciation of their central importance.

Satisfaction of the self-esteem need leads to feelings of self-confidence, worth, strength, capability and adequacy of being useful and necessary in the world. But thwarting of these needs produces feelings of inferiority, of weakness and of helplessness. These feelings in turn give rise to either basic discouragement or else compensatory or neurotic trends. An appreciation of the necessity of basic self-confidence and an understanding of how helpless people are without it, can be easily gained from a study of severe traumatic neurosis (8).[7]

The need for self-actualization. -- Even if all these needs are satisfied, we may still often (if not always) expect that a new discontent and restlessness will soon develop, unless the individual is doing what he is fitted for. A musician must make music, an artist must paint, a poet must write, if he is to be ultimately happy. What a man *can* be, he *must* be. This need we may call self-actualization.

This term, first coined by Kurt Goldstein, is being used in this paper in a much more specific and limited fashion. It refers to the desire for self-fulfillment, namely, to the tendency for him to become actualized in what he is potentially. This tendency might be phrased as the desire to become more and more what one is, to become everything that one is capable of becoming.[p. 383]

The specific form that these needs will take will of course vary greatly from person to person. In one individual it may take the form of the desire to be an ideal mother, in another it may be expressed athletically, and in still another it may be expressed in painting pictures or in inventions. It is not necessarily a creative urge although in people who have any capacities for creation it will take this form.

The clear emergence of these needs rests upon prior satisfaction of the physiological, safety, love and esteem needs. We shall call people who are satisfied in these needs, basically satisfied people, and it is from these that we may expect the fullest (and healthiest) creativeness.[8] Since, in our society, basically satisfied people are the exception, we do not know much about self-actualization, either experimentally or clinically. It remains a challenging problem for research.

The preconditions for the basic need satisfactions. -- There are certain conditions which are immediate prerequisites for the basic need satisfactions. Danger to these is reacted to almost as if it were a direct danger to the basic needs themselves. Such conditions as freedom to speak, freedom to do what one wishes so long as no harm is done to others, freedom to express one's self, freedom to investigate and seek for information, freedom to defend one's self, justice, fairness, honesty, orderliness in the group are examples of such preconditions for basic need satisfactions. Thwarting in these freedoms will be reacted to with a threat or emergency response. These conditions are not ends in themselves but they are *almost* so since they are so closely related to the basic needs, which are apparently the only ends in themselves. These conditions are defended because without them the basic satisfactions are quite impossible, or at least, very severely endangered.[p. 384]

If we remember that the cognitive capacities (perceptual, intellectual, learning) are a set of adjustive tools, which have, among other functions, that of satisfaction of our basic needs, then it is clear that any danger to them, any deprivation or blocking of their free use, must also be indirectly threatening to the basic needs themselves. Such a statement is a partial solution of the general problems of curiosity, the search for knowledge, truth and wisdom, and the ever-persistent urge to solve the cosmic mysteries.

We must therefore introduce another hypothesis and speak of degrees of closeness to the basic needs, for we have already pointed out that *any* conscious desires (partial goals) are more or less important as they are more or less close to the basic needs. The same statement may be made for various behavior acts. An act is psychologically important if it contributes directly to satisfaction of basic needs. The less directly it so contributes, or the weaker this contribution is, the less important this act must be conceived to be from the point of view of dynamic psychology. A similar statement may be made for the various defense or coping mechanisms. Some are very directly related to the protection or attainment of the basic needs, others are only weakly and distantly related. Indeed if we wished, we could speak of more basic and less basic defense mechanisms, and then affirm that danger to the more basic defenses is more threatening than danger to less basic defenses (always remembering that this is so only because of their relationship to the basic needs).

The desires to know and to understand. -- So far, we have mentioned the cognitive needs only in passing. Acquiring knowledge and systematizing the universe have been considered as, in part, techniques for the achievement of basic safety in the world, or, for the intelligent man, expressions of self-actualization. Also freedom of inquiry and expression have been discussed as preconditions of satisfactions of the basic needs. True though these formulations may be, they do not constitute definitive answers to the question as to the motivation role of curiosity, learning, philosophizing, experimenting, etc. They are, at best, no more than partial answers.[p. 385]

This question is especially difficult because we know so little about the facts. Curiosity, exploration, desire for the facts, desire to know may certainly be observed easily enough. The fact that they often are pursued even at great cost to the individual's safety is an earnest of the partial character of our previous discussion. In addition, the writer must admit that, though he has sufficient clinical evidence to postulate the desire to know as a very strong drive in intelligent people, no data are available for unintelligent people. It may then be largely a function of relatively high intelligence. Rather tentatively, then, and largely in the hope of stimulating discussion and research, we shall postulate a basic desire to know, to be aware of reality, to get the facts, to satisfy curiosity, or as Wertheimer phrases it, to see rather than to be blind.

This postulation, however, is not enough. Even after we know, we are impelled to know more and more minutely and microscopically on the one hand, and on the other, more and more extensively in the direction of a world philosophy, religion, etc. The facts that we acquire, if they are isolated or atomistic, inevitably get theorized about, and either analyzed or organized or both. This process has been phrased by some as the search for 'meaning.' We shall then postulate a desire to understand, to systematize, to organize, to analyze, to look for relations and meanings.

Once these desires are accepted for discussion, we see that they too form themselves into a small hierarchy in which the desire to know is prepotent over the desire to understand. All the characteristics of a hierarchy of prepotency that we have described above, seem to hold for this one as well.

We must guard ourselves against the too easy tendency to separate these desires from the basic needs we have discussed above, *i.e.*, to make a sharp dichotomy between 'cognitive' and 'conative' needs. The desire to know and to understand are themselves conative, i.e., have a striving character, and are as much personality needs as the 'basic needs' we have already discussed (19).[p. 386]

III. FURTHER CHARACTERISTICS OF THE BASIC NEEDS

The degree of fixity of the hierarchy of basic needs. -- We have spoken so far as if this hierarchy were a fixed order but actually it is not nearly as rigid as we may have implied. It is true that most of the people with whom we have worked have seemed to have these basic needs in about the order that has been indicated. However, there have been a number of exceptions.

(1) There are some people in whom, for instance, self-esteem seems to be more important than love. This most common reversal in the hierarchy is usually due to the development of the notion that the person who is most likely to be loved is a strong or powerful person, one who inspires respect or fear, and who is self-confident or aggressive. Therefore such people who lack love and seek it, may try hard to put on a front of aggressive, confident behavior. But essentially they seek high self-esteem and its behavior expressions more as a means-to-an-end than for its own sake; they seek self-assertion for the sake of love rather than for self-esteem itself.

(2) There are other, apparently innately creative people in whom the drive to creativeness seems to be more important than any other counter-determinant. Their creativeness might appear not as self-actualization released by basic satisfaction, but in spite of lack of basic satisfaction.

(3) In certain people the level of aspiration may be permanently deadened or lowered. That is to say, the less pre-potent goals may simply be lost, and may disappear forever, so that the person who has experienced life at a very low level, *i. e.*, chronic unemployment, may continue to be satisfied for the rest of his life if only he can get enough food.

(4) The so-called 'psychopathic personality' is another example of permanent loss of the love needs. These are people who, according to the best data available (9), have been starved for love in the earliest months of their lives and have simply lost forever the

desire and the ability to give and to receive affection (as animals lose sucking or pecking reflexes that are not exercised soon enough after birth).[p. 387]

(5) Another cause of reversal of the hierarchy is that when a need has been satisfied for a long time, this need may be under evaluated. People who have never experienced chronic hunger are apt to underestimate its effects and to look upon food as a rather unimportant thing. If they are dominated by a higher need, this higher need will seem to be the most important of all. It then becomes possible, and indeed does actually happen, that they may, for the sake of this higher need, put themselves into the position of being deprived in a more basic need. We may expect that after a long-time deprivation of the more basic need there will be a tendency to reevaluate both needs so that the more pre-potent need will actually become consciously prepotent for the individual who may have given it up very lightly. Thus, a man who has given up his job rather than lose his self-respect, and who then starves for six months or so, may be willing to take his job back even at the price of losing his a self-respect.

(6) Another partial explanation of *apparent* reversals is seen in the fact that we have been talking about the hierarchy of prepotency in terms of consciously felt wants or desires rather than of behavior. Looking at behavior itself may give us the wrong impression. What we have claimed is that the person will want the more basic of two needs when deprived in both. There is no necessary implication here that he will act upon his desires. Let us say again that there are many determinants of behavior other than the needs and desires.

(7) Perhaps more important than all these exceptions are the ones that involve ideals, high social standards, high values and the like. With such values people become martyrs; they give up everything for the sake of a particular ideal, or value. These people may be understood, at least in part, by reference to one basic concept (or

hypothesis) which may be called 'increased frustration-tolerance through early gratification'. People who have been satisfied in their basic needs throughout their lives, particularly in their earlier years, seem to develop exceptional power to withstand present or future thwarting of these needs simply because they have strong,[p. 388] healthy character structure as a result of basic satisfaction. They are the 'strong' people who can easily weather disagreement or opposition, who can swim against the stream of public opinion and who can stand up for the truth at great personal cost. It is just the ones who have loved and been well loved, and who have had many deep friendships who can hold out against hatred, rejection or persecution.

I say all this in spite of the fact that there is a certain amount of sheer habituation which is also involved in any full discussion of frustration tolerance. For instance, it is likely that those persons who have been accustomed to relative starvation for a long time, are partially enabled thereby to withstand food deprivation. What sort of balance must be made between these two tendencies, of habituation on the one hand, and of past satisfaction breeding present frustration tolerance on the other hand, remains to be worked out by further research. Meanwhile we may assume that they are both operative, side by side, since they do not contradict each other, in respect to this phenomenon of increased frustration tolerance, it seems probable that the most important gratifications come in the first two years of life. That is to say, people who have been made secure and strong in the earliest years, tend to remain secure and strong thereafter in the face of whatever threatens.

Degree of relative satisfaction. -- So far, our theoretical discussion may have given the impression that these five sets of needs are somehow in a step-wise, all-or-none relationships to each other. We have spoken in such terms as the following: "If one need is satisfied, then another emerges." This statement might give the false impression that a need must be satisfied 100 per cent before the next need emerges. In actual fact, most members of our society who are normal, are partially satisfied in all their basic needs and partially unsatisfied in all their basic needs at the same time. A more realistic description of the hierarchy would be in terms of decreasing percentages of satisfaction as we go up the hierarchy of prepotency, For instance, if I may assign arbitrary figures for the sake of illustration, it is as if the average citizen [p. 389] is satisfied perhaps 85 per cent in his physiological needs, 70 per cent in his safety needs, 50 per cent in his love needs, 40 per cent in his self-esteem needs, and 10 per cent in his self-actualization needs.

As for the concept of emergence of a new need after satisfaction of the prepotent need, this emergence is not a sudden, saltatory phenomenon but rather a gradual emergence by slow degrees from nothingness. For instance, if prepotent need A is satisfied only 10 per cent: then need B may not be visible at all. However, as this need A becomes satisfied 25 per cent, need B may emerge 5 per cent, as need A becomes satisfied 75 per cent need B may emerge go per cent, and so on.

Unconscious character of needs. -- These needs are neither necessarily conscious nor unconscious. On the whole, however, in the average person, they are more often unconscious rather than conscious. It is not necessary at this point to overhaul the tremendous mass of evidence which indicates the crucial importance of unconscious motivation. It would by now be expected, on a priori grounds alone, that unconscious motivations would on the whole be rather more important than the conscious motivations. What we have called the basic needs are very often largely unconscious although they may, with suitable techniques, and with sophisticated people become conscious.

Cultural specificity and generality of needs. -- This classification of basic needs makes some attempt to take account of the relative unity behind the superficial differences in specific desires from one culture to another. Certainly in any particular culture an individual's conscious motivational content will usually be extremely different from the conscious motivational content of an individual in another society. However, it is the common experience of anthropologists that people, even in different societies, are much more alike than we would think from our first contact with them, and that as we know them better we seem to find more and more of this commonness, We then recognize the most startling differences to be superficial rather than basic, *e. g.*, differences in style of hair-dress, clothes, tastes in food, etc. Our classification of basic [p. 390] needs is in part an attempt to account for this unity behind the apparent diversity from culture to culture. No claim is made that it is ultimate or universal for all cultures. The claim is made only that it is relatively *more* ultimate, more universal, more basic, than the superficial conscious desires from culture to culture, and makes a somewhat closer approach to common-human characteristics, Basic needs are *more* common-human than superficial desires or behaviors.

Multiple motivations of behavior. -- These needs must be understood not to be *exclusive* or single determiners of certain kinds of behavior. An example may be found in any behavior that seems to be physiologically motivated, such as eating, or sexual play or the like. The clinical psychologists have long since found that any behavior may be a channel through which flow various determinants. Or to say it in another way, most behavior is multi-motivated. Within the sphere of motivational determinants any behavior tends to be determined by several or *all* of the basic needs simultaneously rather than by only one of them. The latter would be more an exception than the former. Eating may be partially for the sake of filling the stomach, and partially for the sake of comfort and amelioration of other needs. One may make love not only for pure sexual release, but also to convince one's self of one's masculinity, or to make a conquest, to feel powerful, or to win more basic affection. As an illustration, I may point out that it would be possible (theoretically if not practically) to analyze a single act of an individual and see in it the expression of his physiological needs, his safety needs, his love needs, his esteem needs and self-actualization. This contrasts sharply with the more naive brand of trait psychology in which one trait or one motive accounts for a certain kind of act, *i. e.*, an aggressive act is traced solely to a trait of aggressiveness.

Multiple determinants of behavior. -- Not all behavior is determined by the basic needs. We might even say that not all behavior is motivated. There are many determinants of behavior other than motives.[9] For instance, one other important -[p. 391] class of determinants is the so-called 'field' determinants. Theoretically, at least, behavior may be determined completely by the field, or even by specific isolated external stimuli, as in association of ideas, or certain conditioned reflexes. If in response to the stimulus word 'table' I immediately perceive a memory image of a table, this response certainly has nothing to do with my basic needs.

Secondly, we may call attention again to the concept of 'degree of closeness to the basic needs' or 'degree of motivation.' Some behavior is highly motivated, other behavior is only weakly motivated. Some is not motivated at all (but all behavior is determined).

Another important point [10] is that there is a basic difference between expressive behavior and coping behavior (functional striving, purposive goal seeking). An expressive behavior does not try to do anything; it is simply a reflection of the personality. A stupid man behaves stupidly, not because he wants to, or tries to, or is motivated to, but simply because he is what he is. The same is true when I speak in a bass voice rather than tenor or soprano. The random movements of a healthy child, the smile on the face of a happy man even when he is alone, the springiness of the healthy man's walk, and the erectness of his carriage are other examples of expressive, non-functional behavior. Also the *style* in which a man carries out almost all his behavior, motivated as well as unmotivated, is often expressive.

We may then ask, is *all* behavior expressive or reflective of the character structure? The answer is 'No.' Rote, habitual, automatized, or conventional behavior may or may not be expressive. The same is true for most 'stimulus-bound' behaviors. It is finally necessary to stress that expressiveness of behavior, and goal-directedness of behavior are not mutually exclusive categories. Average behavior is usually both.

Goals as centering principle in motivation theory. -- It will be observed that the basic principle in our classification has [p. 392] been neither the instigation nor the motivated behavior but rather the functions, effects, purposes, or goals of the behavior. It has been proven sufficiently by various people that this is the most suitable point for centering in any motivation theory.[11]

Animal- and human-centering. -- This theory starts with the human being rather than any lower and presumably 'simpler' animal. Too many of the findings that have been made in animals have been proven to be true for animals but not for the human being. There is no reason whatsoever why we should start with animals in order to study human motivation. The logic or rather illogic behind this general fallacy of 'pseudo-simplicity' has been exposed often enough by philosophers and logicians as well as by scientists in each of the various fields. It is no more necessary to study animals before one can study man than it is to study mathematics before one can study geology or psychology or biology.

We may also reject the old, naive, behaviorism which assumed that it was somehow necessary, or at least more 'scientific' to judge human beings by animal standards. One consequence of this belief was that the whole notion of purpose and goal was excluded from motivational psychology simply because one could not ask a white rat about his purposes. Tolman (18) has long since proven in animal studies themselves that this exclusion was not necessary.

References

1. ADLER, A. *Social interest*. London: Faber & Faber, 1938.

2. CANNON, W. B. *Wisdom of the body*. New York: Norton, 1932.

3. FREUD, A. *The ego and the mechanisms of defense*. London: Hogarth, 1937.

4. FREUD, S. *New introductory lectures on psychoanalysis*. New York: Norton, 1933.

5. FROMM, E. *Escape from freedom*. New York: Farrar and Rinehart, 1941.

6. GOLDSTEIN, K. *The organism*. New York: American Book Co., 1939.

7. HORNEY, K. *The neurotic personality of our time*. New York: Norton, 1937.

8. KARDINER, A. *The traumatic neuroses of war*. New York: Hoeber, 1941.

9. LEVY, D. M. Primary affect hunger. *Amer. J. Psychiat.*, 1937, 94, 643-652.

10. MASLOW, A. H. Conflict, frustration, and the theory of threat. *J. abnorm. (soc.) Psychol.*, 1943, 38, 81-86.

11. ----------. Dominance, personality and social behavior in women. *J. soc. Psychol.*, 1939, 10, 3-39.

12. ----------. The dynamics of psychological security-insecurity. *Character & Pers.*, 1942, 10, 331-344.

13. ----------. A preface to motivation theory. *Psychosomatic Med.*, 1943, 5, 85-92.

14. ----------. & MITTLEMANN, B. *Principles of abnormal psychology*. New York: Harper & Bros., 1941.

15. MURRAY, H. A., *et al. Explorations in Personality*. New York: Oxford University Press, 1938.

16. PLANT, J. *Personality and the cultural pattern*. New York: Commonwealth Fund, 1937.

17. SHIRLEY, M. Children's adjustments to a strange situation. *J. Abnorm. Soc. Psychol.*, 1942, 37, 201-217.

18. TOLMAN, E. C. *Purposive behavior in animals and men*. New York: Century, 1932.

19. WERTHEIMER, M. Unpublished lectures at the New School for Social Research.

20. YOUNG, P. T. *Motivation of behavior*. New York: John Wiley & Sons, 1936.

Motivation and the theory of psychopathogenesis. -- The conscious motivational content of everyday life has, according to the foregoing, been conceived to be relatively important or unimportant accordingly as it is more or less closely related to the basic goals. A desire for an ice cream cone might actually be an indirect expression of a desire for love. If it is, then this desire for the ice cream cone becomes extremely important motivation. If however the ice cream is simply something to cool the mouth with, or a casual appetitive reaction, then the desire is relatively unimportant. Everyday conscious desires are to be regarded as symptoms, as [p. 393] *surface indicators of more basic needs*. If we were to take these superficial desires at their face value we would find ourselves in a state of complete confusion which could never be resolved, since we would be dealing seriously with symptoms rather than with what lay behind the symptoms.

Thwarting of unimportant desires produces no psychopathological results; thwarting of a basically important need does produce such results. Any theory of psychopathogenesis must then be based on a sound theory of motivation. A conflict or a frustration is not necessarily pathogenic. It becomes so only when it threatens or thwarts the basic needs, or partial needs that are closely related to the basic needs (10).

The role of gratified needs. -- It has been pointed out above several times that our needs usually emerge only when more prepotent needs have been gratified. Thus gratification has an important role in motivation theory. Apart from this, however, needs cease to play an active determining or organizing role as soon as they are gratified.

What this means is that, *e. g.*, a basically satisfied person no longer has the needs for esteem, love, safety, etc. The only sense in which he might be said to have them is in the almost metaphysical sense that a sated man has hunger, or a filled bottle has emptiness. If we are interested in what *actually* motivates us, and not in what has, will, or might motivate us, then a satisfied need is not a motivator. It must be considered for all practical purposes simply not to exist, to have disappeared. This point should be emphasized because it has been either overlooked or contradicted in every theory of motivation I know.[12] The perfectly healthy, normal, fortunate man has no sex needs or hunger needs, or needs for safety, or for love, or for prestige, or self-esteem, except in stray moments of quickly passing threat. If we were to say otherwise, we should also have to aver that every man had all the pathological reflexes, *e. g.*, Babinski, etc., because if his nervous system were damaged, these would appear.

It is such considerations as these that suggest the bold [p. 394] postulation that a man who is thwarted in any of his basic needs may fairly be envisaged simply as a sick man. This is a fair parallel to our designation as 'sick' of the man who lacks vitamins or minerals. Who is to say that a lack of love is less important than a lack of vitamins? Since we know the pathogenic effects of love starvation, who is to say that we are invoking value-questions in an unscientific or illegitimate way, any more than the physician does who diagnoses and treats pellagra or scurvy? If I were permitted this usage, I should then say simply that a healthy man is primarily motivated by his needs to develop and actualize his fullest potentialities and capacities. If a man has any other basic needs in any active, chronic sense, then he is simply an unhealthy man. He is as surely sick as if he had suddenly developed a strong salt-hunger or calcium hunger.[13]

If this statement seems unusual or paradoxical the reader may be assured that this is only one among many such paradoxes that will appear as we revise our ways of looking at man's deeper motivations. When we ask what man wants of life, we deal with his very essence.

IV. SUMMARY

21. ----------. The experimental analysis of appetite. *Psychol. Bull.*, 1941, 38, 129-164.

(1) There are at least five sets of goals, which we may call basic needs. These are briefly physiological, safety, love, 'esteem, and self-actualization. In addition, we are motivated by the desire to achieve or maintain the various conditions upon which these basic satisfactions rest and by certain more intellectual desires.

(2) These basic goals are related to each other, being arranged in a hierarchy of prepotency. This means that the most prepotent goal will monopolize consciousness and will tend of itself to organize the recruitment of the various capacities of the organism. The less prepotent needs are [p. 395] minimized, even forgotten or denied. But when a need is fairly well satisfied, the next prepotent ('higher') need emerges, in turn to dominate the conscious life and to serve as the center of organization of behavior, since gratified needs are not active motivators.

Thus man is a perpetually wanting animal. Ordinarily the satisfaction of these wants is not altogether mutually exclusive, but only tends to be. The average member of our society is most often partially satisfied and partially unsatisfied in all of his wants. The hierarchy principle is usually empirically observed in terms of increasing percentages of non-satisfaction as we go up the hierarchy. Reversals of the average order of the hierarchy are sometimes observed. Also it has been observed that an individual may permanently lose the higher wants in the hierarchy under special conditions. There are not only ordinarily multiple motivations for usual behavior, but in addition many determinants other than motives.

(3) Any thwarting or possibility of thwarting of these basic human goals, or danger to the defenses which protect them, or to the conditions upon which they rest, is considered to be a psychological threat. With a few exceptions, all psychopathology may be partially traced to such threats. A basically thwarted man may actually be defined as a 'sick' man, if we wish.

(4) It is such basic threats which bring about the general emergency reactions.

(5) Certain other basic problems have not been dealt with because of limitations of space. Among these are (a) the problem of values in any definitive motivation theory, (b) the relation between appetites, desires, needs and what is 'good' for the organism, (c) the etiology of the basic needs and their possible derivation in early childhood, (d) redefinition of motivational concepts, *i. e.*, drive, desire, wish, need, goal, (e) implication of our theory for hedonistic theory, (f) the nature of the uncompleted act, of success and failure, and of aspiration-level, (g) the role of association, habit and conditioning, (h) relation to the [p. 396] theory of inter-personal relations, (i) implications for psychotherapy, (j) implication for theory of society, (k) the theory of selfishness, (l) the relation between needs and cultural patterns, (m) the relation between this theory and Alport's theory of functional autonomy. These as well as certain other less important questions must be considered as motivation theory attempts to become definitive.

Notes

[1] As the child grows up, sheer knowledge and familiarity as well as better motor development make these 'dangers' less and less dangerous and more and more manageable. Throughout life it may be said that one of the main conative functions of education is this neutralizing of apparent dangers through knowledge, *e. g.*, I am not afraid of thunder because I know something about it.

[2] A 'test battery' for safety might be confronting the child with a small exploding firecracker, or with a bewhiskered face; having the mother leave the room, putting him upon a high ladder, a hypodermic injection, having a mouse crawl up to him, etc. Of course I cannot seriously recommend the deliberate use of such

www.ingramcontent.com/pod-product-compliance
Lightning Source LLC
Chambersburg PA
CBHW021441210526
45463CB00002B/604

'tests' for they might very well harm the child being tested. But these and similar situations come up by the score in the child's ordinary day-to-day living and may be observed. There is no reason why those stimuli should not be used with, for example, young chimpanzees.

[3] Not all neurotic individuals feel unsafe. Neurosis may have at its core a thwarting of the affection and esteem needs in a person who is generally safe.

[4] For further details see (12) and (16, Chap. 5).

[5] Whether or not this particular desire is universal we do not know. The crucial question, especially important today, is "Will men who are enslaved and dominated inevitably feel dissatisfied and rebellious?" We may assume on the basis of commonly known clinical data that a man who has known true freedom (not paid for by giving up safety and security but rather built on the basis of adequate safety and security) will not willingly or easily allow his freedom to be taken away from him. But we do not know that this is true for the person born into slavery. The events of the next decade should give us our answer. See discussion of this problem in (5).

[6] Perhaps the desire for prestige and respect from others is subsidiary to the desire for self-esteem or confidence in oneself. Observation of children seems to indicate that this is so, but clinical data give no clear support for such a conclusion.

[7] For more extensive discussion of normal self-esteem, as well as for reports of various researches, see (11).

[8] Clearly creative behavior, like painting, is like any other behavior in having multiple, determinants. It may be seen in 'innately creative' people whether they are satisfied or not, happy or unhappy, hungry or sated. Also it is clear that creative activity

may be compensatory, ameliorative or purely economic. It is my impression (as yet unconfirmed) that it is possible to distinguish the artistic and intellectual products of basically satisfied people from those of basically unsatisfied people by inspection alone. In any case, here too we must distinguish, in a dynamic fashion, the overt behavior itself from its various motivations or purposes.

[9] I am aware that many psychologists and psychoanalysts use the term 'motivated' and 'determined' synonymously, *e. g.*, Freud. But I consider this an obfuscating usage. Sharp distinctions are necessary for clarity of thought, and precision in experimentation.

[10] To be discussed fully in a subsequent publication.

[11] The interested reader is referred to the very excellent discussion of this point in Murray's *Explorations in Personality* (15).

[12] Note that acceptance of this theory necessitates basic revision of the Freudian theory.

[13] If we were to use the word 'sick' in this way, we should then also have to face squarely the relations of man to his society. One clear implication of our definition would be that (1) since a man is to be called sick who is basically thwarted, and (2) since such basic thwarting is made possible ultimately only by forces outside the individual, then (3) sickness in the individual must come ultimately from sickness in the society. The 'good' or healthy society would then be defined as one that permitted man's highest purposes to emerge by satisfying all his prepotent basic needs.